Jesuits in Profile

Jesuits in Profile
Alive and Well in the U.S.

Craig Boly SJ
September, 1992

edited by Craig Boly, S.J.
photographs by Brad Reynolds, S.J.

A Campion Book

Loyola University Press
Chicago

©1992 Loyola University Press
All rights reserved
Printed in the United States of America

Loyola University Press
3441 North Ashland Avenue
Chicago, Illinois 60657

Library of Congress Cataloging-in-Publication data
Jesuits in profile: alive and well in the U.S./ Craig Boly, S.J., editor
      p. cm.
    1. Jesuits. I. Boly, Craig S., 1944-
BX3706.2.J47 1992
255'.53--dc20   92-5044
                    CIP

Acknowledgment
Cover and interior design by Nancy Gruenke

Contents

Preface

This book of essays takes its genealogy from Ignatius of Loyola, who was reluctant to tell his own story.

These essays are the sometimes reluctant stories of Jesuits from the Oregon province: priests and brothers from Washington, Oregon, Idaho, Montana, and Alaska. They are reprinted here from publications meant originally for Jesuit eyes only. Written shortly before the twin Ignatian anniversaries in 1991— the 500th year of his birth and the 450th year of the founding of the Society of Jesus—the stories in this volume reflect the reticence of Ignatius to talk much about himself.

The first companions of Ignatius realized that God privileged him with astonishing gifts of grace—familiarity with the Trinity in prayer, intimacy with Christ on the mission to labor for the kingdom of God.

Despite the urging of his closest friends, Ignatius refused to talk about his own conversion experience or life of prayer, going so far as to destroy almost all of his spiritual journals. It was not until barely three years before his death on July 31, 1556, that he began narrating a third person account of his life to his secretary, Luis Gonzalez de Camara.

This treasured account of the life of Ignatius is called simply in Jesuit circles *The Autobiography.* In his story, we learn that reading the lives of the saints transformed him, provided him with a new horizon of life, and challenged him about the exalted destiny of service of Christ our Lord.

This awareness has become part of the Jesuit heritage. Ignatius preferred reticence about his own gifts yet realized that the story of other heroes had provoked his own desire. It was only right to tell his story, especially if it would encourage others and give greater glory to God.

This awareness of thanksgiving to God and desire for service explains how this book came about.

In response to an invitation to tell their story, Jesuits from the Northwest of the United States answered a request given by Tom Royce, S.J., the Oregon provincial, beginning in the lenten season of 1985. Letters went out from the provincial inviting various men to write their personal experience on a given theme.

The choice of the first theme for these Jesuit narratives stemmed from a concern of the provincial. In preparation for a gathering of the Oregon province at the June 1985 ordinations in Seattle, the theme selected was "the Spiritual Exercises in the work of Jesuits." The impetus for this topic arose from the provincial's desire to encourage a resurgence of directed retreats in everyday life.

Jesuits from ministries as diverse as Native American missions, high school teaching, university administration, prison chaplaincy, community organizing, and pastoral counseling reflected about how the Exercises of Ignatius animated their work.

Thus was begun a yearly cooperative project by northwest Jesuits to write their own story during Lent on topics chosen for the summer's gathering at ordination. The essays were collected each spring in a small book entitled *Laborers in the Harvest.*

In chronological succession, additional topics were treated. In 1986, essays about the relation between community living and how it affects our mission were added. In 1987, the essays looked at how spiritual direction helps the individual priest or brother in his everyday spiritual life. A fourth volume in 1988 expanded on experiences of solidarity with the poor. A fifth collection of stories the following year recalled the experience of the origin of vocation to priesthood and religious life. The most recent volume in 1990 traced the story of chastity as a fruitful love.

In the following pages, you will look through a variety of windows into the experiences of ordinary men of faith. These anecdotal accounts homestead a whole landscape of personal heartland. Perhaps what stirs the heart most about the stories radiates from a revelation of personal limits, from disclosure not of sufficiency but of desire for God. See if you do not recognize your own story in these honest and generous reflections.

Craig Boly, S.J.
Spokane, Washington

Jesuits in Profile

*I fell in love with God, and to my shy, introverted surprise
I learned that at the core of my being I loved and needed
my Jesuit brothers in community beyond all measure.
Andy Dufner, S.J.*

Challenging to the Max
Andy Dufner, S.J.

My vocation to be a Jesuit came to me on a long and winding path. It's still going on, partly in continuity with the past, partly as different as each day's challenge to serve is unlike the day before.

It started when I was a little kid, maybe five or six years old. In the early morning light of the Montana summers I used to stand on the path to the outhouse and contemplate the growing dawn with soul-swelling awe—my first conscious experience of prayer. God was richly present to me then, just as today.

As a young person I was never attracted to the notion of being a priest. What I saw the priests doing was not something I felt attracted to doing myself. In fact when once a summer school teacher told us children that God gave some people the grace never to fall in love with anyone, and they were called to be priests, I was completely put off by it. How strange, my young mind thought, How can that possibly be right? Happily, it wasn't.

My vocational call really came with my exposure to Jesuits, beginning with our family's move to Spokane, when I was starting my junior year in high school. There we had retreats, where the vocational issue was put right up front: "If you have the basic qualifications"—which in those days were something like two arms, two legs, and a nose—"Maybe YOU TOO are called to be a priest. Think about it!" Well, I thought about it, and it made me sort of sick to my stomach. But God has ways as unique as each one of us. By the time I was a junior at Gonzaga University I knew that I had to face the issue squarely and honestly. It was time either to apply to graduate school or apply to the Jesuits. I spent about half a year saying every prayer I could find and doing every penance or pious practice I could think of to wrest a divine telegram from God that would announce that GOD'S WILL FOR YOU IS ———. It didn't happen, but I got something better: divine indifference.

With crystal clarity, at the end of the novena of grace at St. Aloysius Church, I came to understand that I could do whatever I wanted, and God would still love me all the same. I was flooded with an amazed joy at such unconditional love. I still am today. But okay, God, if you had just the tiniest bit of a leaning one way or the other, which way would it be? "Well, if you went to the Jesuit novitiate and then found out that you didn't like it, what would you have lost? You could then go on to graduate school and get married." Good thinking, God! How simple. Play out all the options. That appealed to me.

I went, I tried it, and I loved it. I still do. I even came to like the service role of being priest for others. I fell in love with God, and to my shy, introverted surprise I learned that at the core of my being I loved and needed my Jesuit brothers in community beyond all measure. And the bonus is I still went to graduate school, and I did fall in love—more than once. Challenging? For me, to the max. Difficult? At times about as much suffering as I thought I could bear. Fulfilling? Yes, I simply wouldn't trade my Jesuit vocation for anything else in the world. Thank you, God. There is nothing quite like being called to be yourself. ✝

We need the sun and the rain from on high, but we also need the soil and the earth and those who are close to it.
Jack Morris, S.J.

Just a Chicken Man
Jack Morris, S.J.

When we unroll the scroll of our yesterdays we're often intrigued
by what sticks, what we remember, what is printed on the exposed
lines. So often it is a surprise moment or event, out of keeping
with the ordinary onflow of daily life. Surprise, as we know, is
one important index for the blazing entrance of the Holy Spirit.

I'd like to recall one such memory, a day during the spring of
my first year in the novitiate in 1950. I had a dental appointment
in Portland. For my return trip to Sheridan, the site of the Oregon
province novitiate some seventy miles southwest of Portland,
I chose to hitchhike, which I had done a great deal of before
joining the Society. The day was sunny and warm. I felt life
everywhere. My raised thumb, however, had no power over all
those sleek, modern cars whizzing by, but it did bring to a halt
what some might call "an old tin lizzy." As it drew to a stop I
noticed rickety, feathery mesh coops helter-skelter in the back
end, almost ready to tumble out.

"Howdy! Just push those things aside," said the driver. He
kept both bulky hands on the wheel and pulled out. After a few
pleasantries I knew that Jed Walton and his wife were, as he said,
"fundamentalist Pentecostal and hold body and soul together
on a small place raisin' chickens." Jed knew that I lived in that
huge, tar-black building above Sheridan and had chosen to follow Jesus in a Catholic religious order. I told him about our vows
and way of life, realizing how strange it must sound to the uned-
ucated, rural chicken man. A wrinkled silence fell between us.

Jed finally looked over and asked, "Do they let you pray alone
up there, or is there always someone watchin'?" I responded. He
went on, "That business about not gettin' married. I don't mean
to be offensive, but it's got the sound of a rusty nail to me. If you
don't mind I'd like to offer you some words."

I looked his way, caught his blue eyes, bright in contrast to his
weathered, wrinkled face. I didn't respond verbally. Jed went on,
"I've been alive a lot longer than you and know somethin' of the
Lord's ways. I also know that God made a man and a woman. At
times life gets hard, real hard, and a woman is a mighty fine

comfort to a man. It ain't just the comfort either. It's about having a home and knowin' where you're goin'. To put it straight in front of you, I don't think I could get along without my Sarah."

"The Bible," Jed continued, "tells us about vows. You're puttin' yourself right there in front of God in all his holiness, and once you speak a vow your word clings to him—you can never take it back. It's mighty serious business. Before you take that vow you'd best throw yourself on your knees and beg your heavenly Father for light, askin' if that's really what he wants you to do. It just ain't right that you don't ask that question before God." Silence again, but now it was bright and fitted right into the goodness of the day itself.

We talked until we got to Sheridan, where I got out. "God bless you," he said. "God bless you," I reciprocated. I watched his old relic pull away and disappear. That was thirty-nine years ago. Jed, just a poor chicken man, gifted me with uniquely powerful words on celibacy and the vows. I always recall with gladness and joy that surprise encounter. Over the years his simple, straightforward wisdom has been there as the single most mem- orable "exhortation" of my novitiate years on both celibacy and the vows. I wonder if God doesn't bless all the poor and marginal of the world with unique gifts. We need the sun and the rain from on high, but we also need the soil and the earth and those who are close to it. We also need to go hitchhiking once in awhile. ✝

*In my felt emptiness and powerlessness,
I had a deep sense of the Lord's own
presence, an abiding presence there
among the poor and marginal that
included myself.*
Patrick B. O'Leary, S. J.

Pathfinding
Patrick B. O'Leary, S.J.

At the close of fourteen graced years of ministry to brother
Jesuits in the early stages of formation, I found myself, on the eve
of a sabbatical, wrestling with a decision about what exactly
I wanted to do. I felt a degree of embarrassment that after
journeying with others in the complexities of prayerful decision
making over many years I found sifting out my own inner movements to be arduous and my vacillating among my possible
choices to be perplexing.

On the one hand, I was drawn to search out a center of
learning where I could open myself to the opportunities for
theological reflection, catch up on my reading, and even write a
little. On the other hand, I felt the pull to the experiential. Years
of reflecting with novices on their experiments among Native
Americans in the Pacific Northwest, with the poor and struggling
people in Central America, with the destitute and homeless
on skid row, with the farm workers in the Willamette Valley,
or with the residents of the L'Arche homes where the "handicapped" are at the heart of the community left in me a hunger
for a kind of knowing that is more direct and immediate. Eventually, I knew that the Lord, for me, was in the hunger.

It wasn't my first venture. In the early seventies, a request
in the Horizons for Justice program for a group experience in
Peru turned out to be a sojourn among four thousand Mayan
Indians in the high country of Guatemala. That was a confrontation with poverty. The poverty was evident in terms of the
simplest of housing: a single room, dirt floor, crude furniture,
and shared accommodations with chickens, goats, and other
friendly members of God's wider family.

But there was a richness in welcome, in affection, in love,
and in acceptance. The poverty I felt most was on my own.
My Spanish was minimal; my Quiche Indian nonexistent.
My urge to do something constructive mounted daily. But all
I really had to give was presence. In my felt emptiness and powerlessness, I had a deep sense of the Lord's own presence,
an abiding presence there among the poor and marginal that

included myself, a presence that was compassionate, loving, intimate, and surprisingly patient and vulnerable.

The return to the area some ten years ago was a different, though complementary, experience. There was again a sense of the Lord's presence, but this time it was more passionate and urgent. It was something tangible in the enthusiasm, the apostolic spirit, and the commitment to liberating service of the Jesuit novices in Panama City. They were bright, dedicated young men in increasing numbers whose contact with and attraction to the Society were inspired by its clear commitment to justice, animated by faith and love.

It was something less explicit, but no less real, in the labors of a Peace Corps volunteer whom I had met in Guatemala and had visited in the mountains of Costa Rica. Janet, nearly seventy, was in her twentieth year of helping to organize co-ops among the poor. She is still generously at it in Guatemala.

It was something so characteristic of the Society in the presidential leadership of the late Caesar Jarez, a former Jesuit provincial or in the scholarly, pastoral commitment to social change so evident in those Jesuits with whom I lived in Managua.

In all the ambiguities of the Nicaraguan revolution, you sensed something in the new hopes of the people—the peasant farmer explaining what it meant to be joined with others working soil that was their own; a mother rejoicing that her children might have access to education and health care; or ordinary laborers participating in the rebuilding of the social, cultural, and political fabric of their country. There was something of the surprise of the Gospel—Jesus present and at ease and daring to break bread with not just the marginal and the poor but also with tax collectors and "sinners."

The experiential sabbatical stretched into two more challenging years at St. Joseph's in Seattle, for which I am more grateful than I can express. Now, once again in an academic setting, I am conscious of the importance of serious and conscientious study. There is great wisdom in Father Pedro Arrupe's comment on discernment: "We find our paths by walking on them." Looking back, I find the movements seem so much clearer and the vacillation far less perplexing. Wonderfully, there is a deeper grasp of the truth Ignatius knew so well: Conversion and transformation rooted in experience and strengthened by reflection and study are a gift to heal and renew both mind and heart. ✞

I feel that it will be the Indian people who will offer a real healing to us Jesuits as we grow poorer and come to own our own brokenness. **Peter Byrne, S.J.**

The Gift of the Poor
Peter Byrne, S.J.

When asked how the Catholic social movement known as the
Catholic Worker started, its founder Dorothy Day replied that
it was all really quite simple. I would say the same thing about
the beginnings of the L'Arche community in Tacoma. It was all
so very simple.

David Rothrock* and I were walking down the alley from the
rectory to the old thirteen-bedroom house where we lived.
It was there that we met Fred Koble and Greg Hannon, two men
with mental handicaps. We asked them if they would join us for
dinner. They agreed, and so we shared our first meal. That was
the beginning; it was as simple as that. The next evening they
appeared at our door at dinner time and shared a second meal.
And on it went, night after night. It was as simple as that. After
a year we asked them to live with us on a permanent basis,
and they gifted us with their presence.

I lived with Fred Koble and Greg Hannon for four good, very
good years. I have not since had a comparable experience. There
were many happy times, a few rough and turbulent times. Fred
and I were very similar; he was a mirror held up to my compul-
sions and my own weaknesses. I learned a great deal from Fred
and Greg. I never had to perform for them. They accepted me
as I was.

My other key experience of being with the poor was a short
stay with the Swinomish Indians during tertianship. I was on
the reservation at La Conner during Lent and the Easter season
of 1981. We often sang "The Lord Hears the Cry of the Poor" at
Mass. When I left the community, the tribal chairman thanked
me for my presence with his people and commented, "Father
Peter, you heard the cry of my people for a priest." Thankfully,
Father Pat Twohy* is with them now.

Something happened to me during the time I spent with these
people. I am easily brought to tears, and the experience still
moves me to the deepest feeling. I took my final vows in the little
Church of St. Paul's Mission on the reservation—on the anniver-
sary of my uncle Neil Byrne's birthday—in order to honor him, to

honor the Jesuits now working with native peoples, and to honor
the Native Americans themselves. I sense on an intuitive level
that I must someday return to them and discover what moved
me so deeply. Moreover, I feel that it will be the Indian people
who will offer a real healing to us Jesuits as we grow poorer
and come to own our own brokenness. ✝

Names marked with an asterisk indicate entries contained in this book. See
Contents for page number.

Living in community with Jesuits of varied ages, theologies, and approaches to life challenged my assumptions about what it meant to be a loving person.
Craig Boly, S.J.

Not Exactly a Necklace of Joy
Craig Boly, S.J.

I grew up in a family of five male siblings. During high school, my dating activities took second place only to sports. I was fascinated with what made women act the way they did. The novitiate with its endless rounds of football, basketball, and handball helped me neglect that fascination—at least until Sunday afternoons when the perfume from women visitors would waft its way up the long cubicle rows during afternoon meditation.

The novitiate taught me how to keep the vow of chastity but said little about how to live it. It wasn't until moving to the college campus at Gonzaga University that issues of attraction and affection and friendship raised new problems for the vow I had taken earlier in a mystical phase of romantic generosity.

All of the vows are about fruitful love—how to serve with a liberated heart. As soon as I was teaching high school during regency at Seattle Preparatory, I realized that the real test of my commitment would come not so much from obedience and poverty as from chastity. Living in community with Jesuits of varied ages, theologies, and approaches to life challenged my assumptions about what it meant to be a loving person. I remember being reprimanded more than once for spending too much time with visiting coeds from other local high schools. My rationalization was that if attractive young women brought their problems to me, it must be an opportunity for apostolic service. What I neglected to consider was what needs of my own the interactions with the women students were meeting.

One thing my Jesuit training did not sufficiently caution me about was being hooked by the neediness of another person. Time after time I would find myself enmeshed in a young woman's problem, because her dilemma would awaken in me my own unfinished business. Attempts at caring would lead to entanglements—I would not know where the other person's problem ended and my involvement started.

Once I was ordained, a whole new realm of loving care came into play through the sacraments. It is almost impossible to describe the depth of consolation I have received to be the one to whom another person has turned for reconciliation. The penitent's humility and faith have opened for me experiences of intimacy with another human being that must be rare even in the best marriages. Through the sacrament of anointing, I have witnessed gracious healings where I was brought into a kind of belonging to families that is like adoption. The priestly sacramental ministry has been fruitful in ways that defy description. Serving the people of God through the Eucharist, the reconciliation, the preaching, the anointing, the baptisms, the weddings, and the funerals—all have generated new life— God's life, in others and in myself.

What do I look for in life? A life of love that includes intimacy and belonging. Chastity has blessed me with the focusing of my affective energies. It has given people access to my life regardless of what they seemed to be able to offer me. This is what I mean by unpossessive love. Because of chastity I do not put any preconditions on whom I will serve. Like a parent, I receive the privilege of nurturing the growth of those who come to me in faith. So instead of regretting the loss of my own children, I feel overwhelmed by the abundant opportunity to parent in the faith my students, my counselees, and my fellow Jesuits.

Of course this does not mean that my life of chastity has been one long beatific pearl necklace of ecstatic joy. My failure in chastity has been a loss of heart in the face of my loneliness, a seeking of respite from the routine of humdrum daily chores, and a quest to reduce anxiety about my worth by eliciting a response of affection and belonging from a special woman friend. My failure in chastity has been a flight from the challenge of demanding male companionship in the Society, a going-it-alone through independence in projects and in seeking recreation free from male competition and jealousy. I can fluctuate between being too cautious or being too reckless. Thank heaven for the Ignatian correctives of the account of conscience, competent spiritual direction, and good friends.

At first I thought this topic was how chastity was a fruitful love for others, how chastity made loving others more blessed and enriching for those to whom I minister. Now I realize that chastity has generated a whole new way of my being in the world. The vow has brought me time and time again to my knees during loneliness, has led me to face what motivates me, and has made me discover the source and horizon of my human project. Chastity has challenged my fluctuating between a grandiose savior mentality and a disposition of flattened collapse. Somewhere in the middle is the Spirit of Jesus breathing the truth of my life into my heart. In prayer, in Jesuit companionship, in ecstatic moments of ministry, it is clear to me that the real fruit of my vow of chastity is my own heart, ripening ever so imperceptibly toward unpossessive love. ✟

The idea that someone—God—had something in mind for me and that there were some people who could help me discover it was deeply appealing.
Peter B. Ely, S.J.

For Almost as Far Back as I Can Remember
Peter B. Ely, S.J.

I am supposed to give a talk in a few days to some young men
interested in finding out more about the Society. I can see them
now looking at me and asking, "Yes, why did you enter the
Jesuits, Father Ely?" Maybe putting down some ideas here will
help me answer that question.

It has been so long I'm not sure I remember accurately. For
almost as far back as I can remember I wanted to be a priest.
I am not sure where that desire came from. It wasn't my mother.
My paternal grandmother died when I was ten and left instruc-
tions that certain of her jewels were to be set in my chalice. But
I didn't know that until much later.

I remember wanting to enter the minor seminary after the
eighth grade and my mother telling me that I (and any other
eighth grader for that matter) was too young to make that decision. The compromise was that I could go to the seminary after
my sophomore year if I still had the desire. When the time came
I didn't have the desire. Then after high school I took steps to
enter St. Edward's Seminary in Seattle to become a diocesan
priest. It became clearer and clearer to me I wanted to be a Jesuit
so, after graduation, I began the process of applying.

I was impressed with my Jesuit teachers in high school. I never
really became close to any of them, but I had the feeling that
some of them, at least, understood me, saw things in me I wasn't
aware of myself. I think that was important. I have always been
moved by those passages in the New Testament where Jesus sees
into people—the woman at the well, Nathaniel, and Peter.

I don't believe it was ever that clear to me in high school who
I was. And the idea that someone—God—had something in mind
for me and that there were some people who could help me
discover it was deeply appealing. When I entered I seemed to
discover more and more about myself. The mystery of myself and
the mystery of God seemed to unfold together. I remember
Father Bill Elliott, our novice master, quoting St. Paul to us once
in a conference in the recreation room at Sheridan, the Oregon

province novitiate, "Your lives are hidden now with Christ in God."

There were times when the hiddenness seemed to have gone too far. I remember at the Mount—the nickname of the philosophy school in Spokane—feeling that I needed to break out of the life of study and structured silence. I remember thinking to myself and, saying to some others, that it was more important to be human than to be a Jesuit, which meant, of course, that I felt my way of living Jesuit life was cutting into my humanness.

Just then I went to regency and found myself in the midst of an apostolically active life. It was wonderful. Suddenly I was responsible for others. How I related to students inside and outside the classroom became the essential thing. Suddenly my personality was a part of my vocation. I found out I was much more of an extrovert than I had ever imagined. All this was deeply confirming of my vocation. To the "hidden with Christ in God" was now added "go preach the Good News."

The final ingredient of vocation was the insight about good works and grace. That came later and not all at once. A key moment was after my second year of theology. I had planned a typical summer of study. The dean of the theologate suggested that I probably needed something else. I didn't know what to do. For months I was in an agony of uncertainty about how to spend my summer. Finally, I was led into an African-American parish in Detroit where I worked as a parish visitor going from home to home talking to people and doing a kind of census.

In terms of something accomplished—credits earned, skills acquired, or courses taught—that summer before ordination was not very worthwhile. But something happened to me. I was only aware of it upon returning for my third year of theology. Being with people who weren't "my kind of people" and not really doing much of anything for them achieved something in me that I had so far missed in all my more planned and focused activity. I began to learn that grace is not the reward of hard work.

Thus, my vocation consists of three ingredients: the interior life—that is, "hidden with Christ in God"—the apostolic life, and the life of grace, which encompasses both the interior life and the apostolic life. Each of these realities has had its moment as my vocation has unfolded. ✝

*What does Jesuit-ness look like when
lived out in the twentieth century, with
its particular social matrices and
particular cultural biases?*
J. K. Adams, S.J.

If I Have Just One Friend
J. K. Adams, S.J.

I had just finished my first full year of the novitiate. We had
welcomed the new class, done a communal discernment about
fall experiments, and I was just days away from leaving for
Missoula where I would spend the next few months at St. Francis
Xavier. My first year as a novice had been long and hard. It had
been a year of unprecedented growth that was accompanied
by unprecedented growing pains. I knew that it was God's hand
that had led me to enter the Society—this growth could not have
happened so dramatically without it. But I was not at all sure that
God intended for me to stay in the Society. It was more than once
that I had my suitcase out, open, and a few articles of clothing
packed. It was more than once that I started fantasizing a future
outside the Society. Now it was the beginning of the second year
when "vow discernment" was the only game in town.

It had been a lonely sort of day, a dark and drizzly Portland
day. That morning I had just finished a novel about a friendship
between two boys. It was a friendship that began as children
and lasted through their adulthood. These friends were totally
dedicated to each other. They would go to any lengths to be
by each other's side. They would love each other no matter what.
It was a sappy novel, but it moved me. I felt two things: first,
the miracle of human relationships and second, deep loneliness.
I felt the lack of such a devoted, dedicated friendship. This was
the feeling that I brought to my evening prayer that night.

Sitting in front of the dying fire in the novitiate library, listening to an Amy Grant record, I was explaining the emptiness that
I felt to the Lord. "Lord," I said, "I think that I need a wife." "But,
Lord," I continued, "if you are calling me to be a Jesuit, then the
only way that I think I can make it is to have just one friend who
I can always count on to be there for me, to hear me and hold me
when I'm scared and lonely, to be willing to listen to me when
I'm hurting, who will celebrate with me, to be bold enough to
confront me when I'm off track, to laugh with me, and to cry with
me. Lord, the only way I can make it is if I have just one friend
who truly loves me." The response that I heard from the Lord is

as close to mystical as I have ever come. It was as real as the fire burning in the fireplace. I heard a voice say, "J.K., can I be that companion?" I knew two things immediately. I knew it was the voice of Jesus. I don't know how I knew, but I knew. And I knew what he meant. It was not just an invitation to any old friendship. It was an invitation to companionship with Jesus in the Society of Jesus.

Many people ask me how I made the choice to become a Jesuit. I could list all kinds of reasons that make sense and are even true. Certainly the influence of Jesuits such as Mike McHugh*, Tom Colgan*, Jack Harrington, and Fred Simoneau in Havre was profound. And there is no doubt that the graces of the Long Retreat, which I still continue to unpack, were essential elements of my decision. It is clear from my conversations with John Fuchs and Rick Ganz* that the reason I made my vows is simply that I was invited.

I no longer ask myself if I should be a Jesuit. But another raging question has replaced it: How shall I be a Jesuit? What does "Jesuit-ness" look like when lived out in me, with a particular history, a particular psychic makeup, a particular way of being in the world? And the question also arises, How shall we be Jesuits? What does Jesuit-ness look like when lived out in the twentieth century, with its particular social matrices and particular cultural biases? But I can never honestly ask again whether I should be a Jesuit. I can never deny that voice that I heard in late September 1986, that voice that gently invited me into a committed friendship with the Lord in this Company that humbly bears his name. ✝

As I watched these parishioners become lectors, adult acolytes, and eucharistic ministers, this young white man from the Pacific Northwest began to understand the healing power of the Word of God. **Phil Boroughs, S.J.**

Vulnerability and Not Competency
Phil Boroughs, S.J.

St. Bernard's, a small African-American parish on Chicago's
South Side, sits amid burned out apartment blocks and litter-
strewn lots in a neighborhood where poverty and crime touch
everyone's life. As a second-year theologian at the Jesuit School
of Theology at Chicago (which has since closed), I joined this
parish in 1976 thinking that eventually I would get involved in
housing issues. However, at the request of the parishioners,
I was asked to facilitate a program to promote lay participation
in liturgical roles. The people explained that they already were
adept at dealing with governmental agencies, but what they
really wanted was greater African-American presence in the
sanctuary of the Church.

Consequently, after working with the parish staff and leadership for several weeks to assess their needs, another scholastic
and I announced at a Sunday liturgy the program that the group
had designed. In the course of the homily, while attempting
to emphasize the importance of lay ministerial roles and lay
responsibility for parish life, I said, "It is up to you people to
make the liturgical life of this parish what you want it to be."

After the liturgy, one of the men of the parish took me aside
and gently but clearly told me that the phrase "you people" was
considered condescending and paternalistic when spoken by
a white person in the African-American community. Embarrassed and apologetic, I resolved to drop that phrase from my
vocabulary. However, the following week, while meeting with
the key leadership of the parish, I used it again. Mortified that
I could be so careless, I stopped my presentation and apologized
to the assembled group. In response, a few people replied that
they weren't offended, and a few others said that they understood my intentions and overlooked it, but the discussion ended
when one woman commented, "Look, if he wants to become
sensitive to our reality, let's not stop him."

Following that meeting and my apology, my relationship with
the people of St. Bernard's parish deepened rapidly, and we
learned from one another. As I watched these parishioners

become lectors, adult acolytes, and eucharistic ministers, this young white man from the Pacific Northwest began to understand the healing power of the Word of God and the radical aspects of the virtue of hope in the midst of overwhelming poverty and oppression.

These memories came back to me a few years later when I was working at St. Leo's parish in Tacoma. After being away from the parish for several months following back surgery, I was visited at the rectory by an elderly woman whom I had never met before. Leaning heavily on her cane and breathing with some difficulty, she slowly entered my office and lowered herself into a chair. When she looked up at me, she asked, "You've been quite sick, haven't you?" When I acknowledged that I had, she said, "Good. Now you'll be able to understand what I need to share with you."

With time and experience I'm learning that it is vulnerability and not just competency, that frequently opens the way for relationships and ministry. ✝

I love the Society; my mind, heart, hopes, and dreams all are formed deeply by this bond of brotherhood, this enduring vision, this present reality.
L. Patrick Carroll, S.J.

The Inability to Imagine Myself Otherwise
L. Patrick Carroll, S.J.

Like everyone who contributes to this volume I have often had
people ask, "When did you decide to be a Jesuit, a priest?"
I invariably answer, "Yesterday." I have made the decision over
and over for thirty-five years. I suspect this will continue.

Ten years ago, in an effort to answer the question more fully,
less flippantly, I wrote (as much for myself as for others), *To Love,
To Serve, To Share: Challenges to a Religious* (Liturgical Press,
1979). I still offer this slim volume to those who seek help in
discerning their own call. Even after ten years this book still
details pretty well why (more importantly to what) I still say
"Yes." Though not a great book, it is an honest one.

Let me acknowledge that my home laid the seeds of my Jesuit/
priestly vocation. My dad had been a Jesuit novice and always
carried with him some guilt for leaving. I inherited a bit of his
longing, a mixed bag with which I had to wrestle mightily before
ordination. Looking back I am grateful he shared this longing
with me.

The neighborhood in which I grew up (St. Joseph's parish
in Seattle) made the choice of a Jesuit seminary very easy, very
natural. Eleven members of my brother's grade school class—
but two years ahead of me—went to Sheridan, the site of the
Oregon province novitiate. After high school almost equal numbers of my friends went to the University of Washington, Seattle
University, or the novitiate. Because I didn't think I could play
basketball at either (at the time), I chose Sheridan. The profound
decision was honored despite my amazingly nonillustrious
academic record, and I was accepted.

My decision/God's call was affirmed many times over the
years, perhaps most critically in 1972 when, after two miserable
years as rector-president at Bellarmine Preparatory in Tacoma,
I tried to resign. Ken Galbraith, the provincial at the time, invited
me to stay, and grow. I now see the decision not to turn back as
critical in the lifetime of choices.

Three challenges have continually raised the question of
vocation for me. Every time a close friend leaves, and there have

been many, I wonder why I stay. Every time the Church as an institution displays its shadow side, I wonder how I can represent it. Specifically, I am in constant pain and doubt about representing officially the Church's discrimination against women; this compromise is always present, always ambiguous. And each time I have fallen in love I have prayerfully had to face my desire to continue this priestly project.

I cannot adequately explain the types of graces that come in each of the above instances. In stillness, with the often vague voice of Jesus still smilingly whispering "come," I simply cannot do otherwise. I love being a priest. I cannot imagine another way of life that would so satisfy the person I have become, am becoming. I love celebrating the Eucharist, often the one thing that makes any sense of life. I love preaching, telling over and over the story of Jesus, which I cannot not believe. I love the involvement in people's lives at birth, at death, and at every moment in between.

Though others depart, I have never been able to say, with any honesty, that I was unhappy, or unfilled, or unfruitful for others or myself.

Though the Church as an institution can often be an embarrassment, a burden more than a help, it will not be better without me. Besides, all its massive faults are only mine, writ large. Also I have been blessed with frequent, even constant experiences of the Church at its best in wonderful communities of faith.

Although I have desired down to my toes to marry, this has never been most truly who I am, nor have I ever felt that I wanted to or could be what the other person—however loved—wanted or needed.

Finally, in another moment of honesty, I admit, to my chagrin, that I am more tied to "priest" than "Jesuit." I love the Society; my mind, heart, hopes, and dreams all are formed deeply by this bond of brotherhood, this enduring vision, this present reality. But yet it is being a priest that most deeply satisfies my heart. The grace of vocation for me, yesterday, today, and, I trust, tomorrow, rests simply in the inability to imagine myself otherwise. I cannot explain this. I can only say "Thanks!" ✝

The typical, routine meeting with spiritual directors has been an opportunity to share my faith and hear an "amen" to my prayer.
Gordon Moreland, S.J.

The Cry of My Heart
Gordon Moreland, S.J.

Father William Gill, S.J., undoubtedly had the greatest impact
of any spiritual director on my life. Part of this was due to the fact
that he directed me when I was just eighteen years old and still
in a most impressionable phase of life. But his influence, I think,
would be just about as great at any age.

I remember vividly the day I first spoke with him at some
length. As he listened to me I saw tears running down his face.
He heard the cry of my heart. His verbal response helped, but
the tears were more important. It is a wonderful experience to
feel that one has been heard at the deepest possible level. On
one occasion, when I saw him approaching the chapel where
I had made an appointment for confession, I had a momentary
impression that it was Christ walking down the hall toward me.
A memorable remark of his was "Gordon, don't be surprised that
you have been so bad. Be thankful that you aren't worse." This
may not sound very complimentary, but it continues to be
encouraging to me.

Once when I was very troubled over the question of vocation
I spoke with Father Barrett Corrigan, the retreat director.
He seemed unable to comprehend what I was talking about.
He was practically speechless. I don't think he knew what to say,
but he treated me with immense respect. That was a great grace
for me.

When I was going through a difficult transition in my spiritual
journey I spoke with a Jesuit priest named Joe O'Connell. He told
me that I had to leave someplace in order to go someplace and
then described Abraham's journey of faith. This was one of the
most important conversations of my life.

While most of my spiritual directors over the years have not
made a dramatic impact that stirs my memory today, many of
them performed well the ministry that Tom Clancy describes
in his book on spiritual conversation. The typical, routine meeting with spiritual directors has been an opportunity to share my
faith and hear an "amen" to my prayer. "It is not good for man
to be alone" (Gen. 2:18). ✤

All my spiritual directors clarified the "assumptive world" I currently occupied, showing me the narrow parameters I had drawn around myself.
Jerry Cobb, S.J.

Spiritual Direction in the Car Wash
Jerry Cobb, S.J.

Lily Tomlin once emerged from a car wash seated atop a car,
with beehive hairdo intact despite the rush of water and rollers.
Holding a can of hairspray in one hand, she announced, "I am
not an actress, I am a real person," and then proceeded to en-
dorse the hairspray. Spiritual direction is similar to this. I am
neither an actor nor an unflappable cleric, but a real human
being who gets buffeted and sprayed and jostled by the movements of various spirits in the life of apostolic discernment.
So I need spiritual direction to support me and educate me about
my life's moments and movements before God.

My spiritual directors over the past ten years had wildly
unique styles. Peter Fleming would purse a cigarette between
his lips, peer over his glasses rather skeptically, and ask, "That
thought?. . . That feeling?. . . What's that gesture?!" Weekly conversations with Peter were freefloating "verbal examens" that
decoded scenes from my life. When I ran out of words I was often
up against a spiritual wall, and Peter would say, "Well, you can
either go through it or back away."

Bob Egan directed me in a gentler but very prophetic fashion,
urging me to get more serious about intellectual and affective
issues. His use of the Enneagram also made me more understanding of people whose fixations differ from my own.

Mario DePaoli taught me that a sense of humor, profound
compassion, and a commitment to regular self-examination
would keep me "processed" about my affectivity and action,
thus preventing emotional staleness in ministry.

Jack Costello had an assured and kind manner of spiritual
direction that supported me through the grief of the death of
my father.

Ken Galbraith helped me survive my Ph.D. comprehensive
exams by working through my own sense of drivenness, perfec-
tionism, and self-doubt.

All my spiritual directors clarified the "assumptive world"
I currently occupied, showing me the narrow parameters I had
drawn around myself. When my throat clenched, hands gripped,

and heart contracted or cooled, they suggested I move to a more expansive world, with better prospects for fruitful ministry and intimacy with divine and human persons.

I still hear them in their several voices:
- "Why is 'making a mark' such a priority? On my deathbed I hope to say I experienced life to the fullest. Who needs more?"
- "Work solidly five days a week and take two days off."
- "Did you become a Jesuit because you have difficulties with intimacy, or do you have difficulties with intimacy because you are a Jesuit?"
- "Exercise for you is not escape; it is highly beneficial."
- "Sounds like 'lonely-priest-scheduling-appointments-at-night-syndrome' to me."
- "You have to ask the question, What will make you happy?"
- "For sure, this is something you will want to pray about."
- "The minister is the ministry."
- "Often Jesuits don't connect with people; it's part of the arrogance of clerical narcissism."
- "When in doubt whether to speak or to be quiet, be quiet and listen."

None of these comments, nor spiritual direction itself, ever sought to preserve my composure like hairspray would hold my thinning hair together. But in weekly conversations with these directors I have consistently—and often dramatically—found God's redeeming voice spelling out for me a happier style of Jesuit living. ✝

Along with novelist Graham Greene I believe that God does not demand anything from us that we cannot give him. **Ed Goldian, S.J.**

It's Never Easy
Ed Goldian, S.J.

A former classmate once told me, "If you don't understand it, I can't explain it to you." My response, years later, are the words of Sun Yat-Sen, "To understand is hard. Once one understands, action is easy." Over the years my understanding has grown and my living of chastity has become, not easy, but easier.

I say not easy because with the vow I did not give up my human nature, my human inclinations. Like the story of the young monk who asked the abbot, "When do temptations against chastity stop?" I know the answer is, "I'm only sixty years old. You'd better ask my brother. He's eighty." I must admit that my only temptation is when witnessing marriages. It's not so much that I desire genital sex. What I do desire is the fruits. I would love to have children.

What I am is sexually abstinent. What I am not is intimately immature. Rather than my psychic wellsprings drying up, they are filled to the rim. In the Society I have two close friends. It was three until John O'Brien left us. Outside I have one other male friend. I have a multitude of female friends with whom I have bonded fully. Like teenagers on a date who have decided ahead of time there will be no sex, we can relax and enjoy one another's company without fear of hurt feelings or broken relationships because we've simply "said no" to sex. We relate so intimately we begin to think alike and when this happens we joke that "we've been married too long."

I think females relate more easily to me because they know I have taken—and keep—the vow, and no physical demands will be made even if human nature sometimes desires otherwise. As I said before, it's getting easier, not easy. For easy translates into, as Alf would proclaim, "no problem." It's easier because I'm fortified daily by the Eucharist, by prayer and discipline, and by community.

And finally the question of priesthood and celibacy arises. Along with many of my Protestant colleagues I agree it is harder to devote oneself to ministry and to family than it is to being celibate. Along with novelist Graham Greene I believe that God does not demand anything from us that we cannot give him. I believe, as I read somewhere recently, that God does not call us and then impose celibacy upon us. He invites those to whom he has already given the gift of celibacy. Celibacy, as the Jesuit theologian Avery Dulles reminds us, is not the problem. Celibacy has been around for centuries and there were many religious vocations, even during times of changing mores. The problem, seen not only in vocations to priesthood/religious life but also in marriage and other human endeavors, is a lack of commitment.

Whether married, single, or in priesthood/religious life, chastity—that is, moral virtue—is the duty of everyone. While never easy, it gets easier the more it is practiced. I rejoice in my maleness, my humanness. Unless I'm on one of my periodic diets, you will never hear me pray "that this too, too solid flesh would melt away." ✝

From Mitch and Gib, I learned to go where the people are, to laugh with them when they're happy, to cry when they're sad, to dance at celebrations, and to share in their feasts. **Tom Connolly, S.J.**

God's Ambassadors
Tom Connolly, S.J.

When I came to St. Michael's in 1953, Indians were the last thing
on my mind. But faced with three years "stuck on the hill"
I joined the search for apostolates which would give me something to do "off the hill." Not pious enough to teach catechism
in the Hillyard neighborhood in Spokane nor athletic enough to
coach at the Catholic grade schools, I finally found my "way off"
when I met Father Dom Doyle. I signed on to help him at the
Indian mission on the Spokane reservation.

Digging a well, building a hall, meeting the folks, watching
stick games—what villa days they were! Then April 14, 1954,
Dom Doyle took me to my first Indian funeral, and I met Mitch
Michael, a jovial old prayer leader from the Coeur d'Alene tribe
in Idaho. It turned out to be the first day of the rest of my life!

Mitch wanted to reprint the old 1880 book of prayers and
hymns. Tattered pages were being recopied by hand, and old
leaders were beginning to die off. He wanted to keep this religious culture alive for another generation. I offered to help
and spent much of my free time with Mitch and his wife Mary
at wakes and celebrations, editing and translating, meeting
elders of four tribes, and sharing in centuries of Indian culture
and hundreds of years of rich Catholic tradition. They took me
into their homes and into their hearts.

After ordination Mitch became a mentor to me, while I
laughed at his stories, traveled with him to funerals and pow-
wows, and incorporated traditional Indian ceremonials into the
liturgy. Mitch had been born in a tepee at Spokane's Indian
Canyon, and he shared with me his warm feelings for his Indian
past. He also shared his pain over the disintegration that so many
forced changes had brought to the lives of his children and
his grandchildren.

Then in 1969 Mitch brought me to Gibson Eli, the last medicine man of the Spokanes. I found rich friendship and another
mentor. In January, Gib invited me to his "medicine dance,"
giving thanks for mystical experiences with spirits of nature
and renewing contact in song and dance with those ancient

angelic forms that brought messages and powers to help heal the people. "God gave this power to the Indians to heal when we had no doctors," said Gib. In time he asked me to travel with him. I sat next to him in the darkened room and helped him sing his power song while he drew sickness out of people. I shared his joy when we saw people smile again or walk easily again.

From Mitch and Gib, I learned to go where the people are, to laugh with them when they're happy, to cry when they're sad, to dance at celebrations, and to share in their feasts. Whenever people were in need, we were there, from Vancouver Island to Montana, calling forth the Holy Spirit and the power of Jesus, and calling on the mystical power of God's ambassadors in the animal world to help bring order into the world of humans.

They were powerful times of heartache and ecstasy, of the richness of an ancient past and of the alcoholism, broken families, and fatal accidents of an uncontrolled fall into the future. But always it was there—some ancient power within, helping one another to survive in a falling-apart world. With Gib Eli, I shared their old testament; with Mitch Michael, I shared their new testament. My two guardians are both gone now, but my whole life has been so much richer because they allowed me to share in their way. ✞

My experience of the Spiritual Exercises is that I am always forgiven and loved. **Tom Colgan, S.J.**

Healing the Nations Is as Close to Jesus' Heart as Healing the Children He Loved

Tom Colgan, S.J.

My apostolate is in the healing ministry, especially in the area of emotional hurts, so reconciliation enters into all my work—reconciliation to self, to God, to others, to systems, and to creation.

My experience of the Spiritual Exercises is that I am always forgiven and loved. In his unconditional love the Lord heals me and others. His love frees me to enjoy being myself as I work and teach others to learn more about his healing love and power. The concluding grace of the First Week is believing from the heart that I am a loved and forgiven sinner.

The experience of the Second Week for me occurs when the Lord changes my heart more into his, that is, more loving and fearless. Accepting Jesus' love, in particular his love for the poor, has meant allowing Jesus and Mary to heal my hidden wounds, to love my poor pathetic "old man," my interior oppressor. In this acceptance I have had to learn to forgive others, to forgive God, and even to forgive creation (it isn't the way I want it).

In the Exercises, our Father has taught me that "social justice" is extending the love and forgiveness I have received. His love is very physical, like healing or the Eucharist. Healing the nations is as close to Jesus' heart as healing the children he loved. I believe to extend healing outwards beyond our nation, beyond our race, and beyond our culture to include all of his children leads to the cross. The historical circumstances of Jesus' cross have parallels today. He was—continues to be—crucified by legitimate government authorities. He was—and is—suffering at the hands of "official" government militaries. He was—and is—suffering and condemned with the fickle acquiescence of the masses. He was put to death by some of the religious leaders of his day. Seeing Jesus suffer at these people's hands has helped to open me to see his sufferings today in parallel situations. The structure of the Exercises gives a solid base to face injustice.

Jesus said, "I am with you always." I believe he does now what he did during his days here on earth: He teaches, heals, reconciles, and faces injustice with real love. ✝

It is the opportunity to apply daily to my work the discernment of spirits as well as the First Principle and Foundation, the Two Standards, and the Contemplation to Attain the Love of God that gives me my best and fullest satisfaction.
J. Kevin Waters, S.J.

The Evil Spirit Brings More Fear Than Faith
J. Kevin Waters, S.J.

Fifteen years after his pilgrimage to Jerusalem, Ignatius urged
Isabel Roser, his long time friend and donor from Paris days,
by letter to discern the spirits before coming to Rome. "The good
spirit," he wrote, "brings strength and hope, and a wonderful
calm. The evil spirit brings strife, restlessness and dread. The evil
spirit brings more fear than faith."

This Ignatian passage, epitomizing for me the Founder's
discernment of spirits, underlays an aria by the Jesuit composer
Ernest Ferlita's and my own opera, *Dear Ignatius, Dear Isabel.*
From the time I set the text in 1977, I have often relied on it for
my own personal decisions and for directing others.

Students, faculty, and program directors seldom frequent
the dean's office simply to bid him good morning. Their appointments are functional, serving the single purpose of solving
problems: "changing my unfair grade" or "one of the teachers
in my department is never here before noon on Mondays nor
here after that time on Fridays."

Sorting through the central justice issues of these wrongs,
seemingly trivial at times, is the task at hand. Rarely does the
plaintiff view the matter to be inconsequential or a hurt to be
borne magnanimously. Nor should I. Hearing the grievances
through, explanatory for me and unburdening for the other,
may help create clarity when it comes time for decision making:
decision about objectivity pertaining to the case that optimally,
in time, will lead to either "letting go" or to achieving rudimen-
tary indifference. When one senses that this kind of positive
climate has been attained, the process of discernment can begin.

If through well-deliberated reflection the question of injustice
becomes either diffused or even begged, the discernment of
spirits can helpfully guide one to the next move. Injustice, at the
other end of the spectrum, also leads to discriminating between
the movements of the heart and the movements of the mind.
Here, as is always the case in matters of the spiritual life,
one must ascertain the level, intensity, comprehension, and

faith of the client. One might begin by considering that primordial symbol of salvation, the Sign of the Cross. We have been baptized with it and through it we find that our every sorrow is capable of merit.

Raw injustice found within the confines of the university can be better handled if some objectivity has been secured from the outset. As experience in this process of comprehending our own affectivity in the face of cruelty widens, it also builds for the client and, for me, creates a reservoir of trust in divine providence.

There is no administrative task that I can undertake where the discernment of spirits would not be an effective tool. If, on the contrary, I hasten my judgment and neglect taking the longer path to discernment, I risk debilitating my own effectiveness in extending faith, peace, and trust.

It is the opportunity to apply daily to my work the discernment of spirits as well as the First Principle and Foundation, the Two Standards, and the Contemplation to Attain the Love of God that gives me my best and fullest satisfaction. ✝

My True-friend does not have much in the way of worldly goods. But what he does have he has given to me.
Pat Conroy, S.J.

Sweat Lodge
Pat Conroy, S.J.

Not long ago I was feeling the burden of my personal sins and the difficulties of my ministry on the reservation. This seems to occur every once in awhile, and often I have been able to find solace and understanding from Brother Jerry Sullivan in Inchelium, Washington. But this day I was in Wellpinit, and Inchelium was hours away.

Fortunately, I was with one of the men, an Indian who has become a True-friend and one who had accepted me as a fellow human being, not only as "Father." As we spoke, it was soon clear to him that I was carrying a heavy burden. He did not say much. "I will help you if I can," he said. "We will sweat."

My True-friend asked me if I minded smoke, intending that I should prepare myself in this manner. He lit the fire to heat the stones, then lit a cigarette for me. As I smoked in silence, the smoke from the fire lifted and gently drifted up, warming the surrounding earth. A steam mist rose from the damp ground. It seemed that all the elements were purifying themselves within me.

Many times we have sweat together, but this time we sweat differently. We pray now not for our families or our loved ones nor for the health of elders or for the safety of youth. This time we pray for a certain one, one in need of forgiveness. Of healing. Of strength.

Once inside the warm darkness, the searing heat enveloped us, and the cleansing sweat poured from my body. It was soon joined by my tears. I sobbed my grief as my True-friend prayed.

"Grandfather, I ask you to enter my partner's heart. Go deep, past the pain. Give him peace and strength."

My True-friend does not have much in the way of worldly goods. His family must live within its means. What he does have he has given to me. His friendship. His prayers. The sweat lodge.

Three times in, three times out we prayed, and when we were finished, my burden was lightened. As I reflect on our time together, I realize that this was not an ordinary time. It was an experience of sacrament; its minister, an Indian man. ✟

In Jesus, God loves me concretely and personally simply because I am who I am. **Michael L. Cook, S.J.**

To Ask How the Spiritual Exercises Animates My Work Is to Ask How Jesus Animates My Work
Michael L. Cook, S.J.

To ask how the Spiritual Exercises animates my work is to ask how Jesus animates my work. When I entered the novitiate at the age of seventeen in 1953, God remained a rather just and exacting God and Jesus a remote and mysterious figure.

The deepest and most influential experience of my Jesuit life has been the first Long Retreat that October under the direction of Bill Elliott. For the first time Jesus came alive for me as a person.

The experience, put most simply, was one of being loved totally and unconditionally. In retrospect, I can analyze it as follows: that in Jesus, God loves me concretely and personally simply because I am who I am—not for anything that I can do but simply for myself—and that God sets no conditions to that love; for example, "I will love you if you live up to certain expectations."

The realization of such love is a tremendously freeing experience. It frees me to love God because God is God and to set no conditions to that love. It frees me to love others because they are who they are, without demanding that they live up to my expectations of who they should be. And finally, most importantly for the spiritual life, it frees me to love myself properly and truly as a gift from the hand of God without trying to live up to false projections of who I should be, whether imposed by others or by my own distorted self-image. It allows me to embrace the gift of life that God has given me, concretely and personally, and it calls me to live that gift to the fullest, to become the person that God has created me to be and not someone else.

Obviously, the above has been and continues to be the project of my whole life. I am still striving to realize concretely and specifically the freedom for which Christ has set us free (Gal. 5:1).

From the time of that first Long Retreat, I knew—however inchoately—that I wanted to be a theologian for one simple reason: I deeply desired to know Jesus more intimately, to love him more ardently, and to follow him more closely.

My great love has always been Christology and especially its scriptural foundations. Over the years my image of Jesus has changed because of such work. I feel it has been purified and deepened.

And it has led me to a deepening realization that the truest and most primary knowledge of Jesus is not to be found in abstract formulae—as useful as they may be—but in actually taking up one's cross and following Jesus on the way.

Today that means entering into the struggles of the Jesus who is poor, marginated, and oppressed. It means, above all, walking with the Jesus who is our sister and who frequently suffers from a double oppression: not only that of class or race but also that of simply being woman. ✟

In all of this I give what I have to give,
which is "Jesus loves all of us and I love
you, too." **Michael McHugh, S.J.**

Past, Present, Future
Michael McHugh, S.J.

When I was a freshman at Seattle Preparatory in 1934, Father
Dom Maruca was the principal. I remember that he talked
about the Jesuit novices at Sheridan and "how poor they lived."
That impressed me. I think the attraction of poverty was one
of the reasons I wanted to join the Jesuits.

Since vows, however, my own attempts to live a poor and
simple life have been mostly sloppy and slipshod, even down-
right clumsy and thoughtless.

Example. I was in the juniorate—it was wartime. My family
gave me a fine but costly fountain pen. They came to visit and
asked how I liked the pen. I said I had handed it in to the Father
Minister. "You did what!?" No appeals of mine to poverty as a
firm wall of religion made any dent. Some family members still
(almost fifty years later) remember that expensive pen I gave
away. Within my Jesuit family I have shown sometimes a prefer-
ential option for the poor contrary to the preferences of the men
I lived with.

Example. I was at St. Ignatius in Portland. I invited back-door
beggars in to share the community meal at the table with us.

Example. I was at St. Jude's in Havre. I appropriated food
and furniture from the Jesuit living quarters to give away to
poor people.

These now seem to have been ill-conceived and inconsider-
ately executed attempts at solidarity with the poor without
solidarity of consent from the community. I apologize for my
abrasive behavior.

So much for the past. What about now? At present I live among
the Blackfeet Indians. Poverty has many faces here. I am seeking
solidarity with the poor in these hopeful ways:
• eating welfare (commodity) foods, as many here have to
• cooking, waiting table, and eating at our community center
  for street people
• going around to people's homes in love, friendship, and
  encouragement

- praying with people
- weeping with those who weep, in their brokenness and bereavement
- sharing all joys, sorrows, hopes, and pain

I go daily (if possible) to Alcoholics Anonymous meetings, to the jail, and to the alcohol treatment center. I do frequent 5th Steps—admitting to God and to ourselves the exact nature of our wrongs—in the A.A. program. I am part of several school support groups for kids who are suffering.

In all of this I give what I have to give, which is "Jesus loves all of us and I love you, too."

So much for my mistakes of the past and the feeble but earnest attempts of the present. What of the future? I've told Father Provincial that I'm happy here, but I'll be willing to work in some caring capacity for AIDS patients—if such an opportunity comes up. ✝

*Sometimes in my work as a college
teacher, when I am having a difficult
time relating to a person, I pause to pray
to the Trinity indwelling there and to
ask for the grace to learn to love that
person as the Lord does.*
Frank Costello, S.J.

"And Makes a Temple of Me" Can Be a Powerful Stimulus to Prayer

Frank Costello, S.J.

In reply to the question about how the Spiritual Exercises animates my work, I want to cite one of the many passages that influence my life and work experience. In the Contemplation for Learning to Love Like God, the Second Point reads:

> This is how to reflect how God dwells in creatures: in the elements giving them existence, in the plants giving them life, in the animals conferring on them sensation, in man bestowing understanding. So He dwells in me and gives me being, life, sensation and intelligence; and makes a temple of me, since I am created in the likeness of the Divine Majesty.

I have discovered in the retreats I have directed for bishops, priests, religious women and men, and for the laity that the phrase "and makes a temple of me" can be a powerful stimulus to prayer. It has been my experience that nearly all the retreatants have a basic, negative self-image. If they are able to see God in all things, especially in themselves as temples of the Holy Spirit, the graces of the retreat lead them to accept themselves in a new and positive way.

I usually try at the liturgy, on the day of this contemplation, to use incense at the preparation of the gifts. I point out to the retreatants that in the Christian tradition only sacred things are incensed such as the altar of sacrifice, the Book of the Gospels, and the Blessed Sacrament exposed. Then, I incense them, reminding them how sacred and holy they are because of their baptismal incorporation into Christ and the dwelling of the Trinity in their bodies.

Sometimes in my work as a college teacher, when I am having a difficult time relating to a person, I pause to pray to the Trinity indwelling there and to ask for the grace to learn to love that person as the Lord does.

It has been my experience that the contemplation, especially the Second Point, can be a powerful grace for me and the people I serve. ✝

The hardest times I have experienced in my apostolic work occurred when I sensed I did not have the support of the community in what I thought I was doing for Christ. **James N. Meehan, S.J.**

My Apostolate Is to Be Christ to My Community and to Let the Community Be Christ to Me
James N. Meehan, S.J.

As I grow older, I find *community* and *apostolate* have become the subject and predicate of my life, ungrammatical as that might be. No personal affirmation means more to me than to affirm being a Jesuit and being part of what the Jesuits are doing.

I have been in many a discernment about how a community should change or not change, about the meaning of *life-style* and *apostolic thrust*. I accept the human conflict involved in this as painful and inevitable, and the memory of this point seems far more stimulating than the process appeared at the time. Still, I recognize that we constantly need to clarify who we are and what we want to do.

I have chosen apostolates but more often have had them chosen for me by the community. And always it was a conscious, self-affirming decision, because I wanted to be part of what the community wanted to do. Never were my spirits so low as during the isolated life of graduate studies—only the desire to be a more useful part of the Jesuit apostolate made me persevere. The hardest times I have experienced in my apostolic work occurred when I sensed I did not have the support of the community in what I thought I was doing for Christ.

What occurs to me now is how much we are actually all one in Christ. My spiritual life has increasingly moved towards a simplifying understanding of how much my apostolate is to be Christ to my community and to let the community be Christ to me. This involves no assumption that the community always chooses the right course, makes the wisest decisions, or follows the truest inspirations. It does involve recognizing that the same Spirit who guides me as a bumbling individual guides the bumbling community.

If awareness of the unifying presence of Christ applies in the fullest sense to everyone, it especially applies in my experience to the wonderful holy sinners I am privileged to call my Jesuit brothers. For me the greatest compliment I can receive from those who have come to know and love me in my apostolic efforts is to hear them say that through me they have come to better understand and appreciate the Jesuits as a Christian community. ✞

There is one unwritten rule in the villages that never goes unheeded: every guest is to be fed, even if it means going a little hungry yourself.
Gene Delmore, S.J.

Hospitality
Gene Delmore, S.J.

I've always taken hospitality for granted in the places I've served, but nowhere is it so keenly felt and needed as in the villages of rural Alaska.

Recently I had gone to Pilot Station in western Alaska for a weekend of ministry, and I had come down with a miserable cold that I couldn't seem to shake. Louise Kelly Britton, parish council president and a "live wire" in the village, called to tell me there was Yukon fiddle music at the community hall and my dancing legs would be welcome. I halfheartedly accepted but said I might get an early bed, for Sunday is my workday. She took that good-naturedly, and I started getting ready for some sack time.

A few minutes went by since Louise called, when her brother Abe gave me a ring and said, "Father, have you eaten yet?" "Well, Abe," I replied, "I had a little soup and that might take care of me till tomorrow." Usually I eat with different families at Pilot Station because the rectory conditions are simple (a hot plate and no running water), and it provides a chance to be with the people. I thought nothing of Abe's call, which came about nine in the evening, when suddenly—within fifteen minutes—I heard four-wheelers approaching the church on the side of the hill. Then footsteps came through the church to the residence. "Knock-knock. Hi, Father, here's some moose soup and bread for your supper." "Thanks," say I, listening to the rumbling beginning in my stomach. Five minutes later, another knock, and more moose soup and bread was delivered. "Wow, thanks, this is great," I said. Three minutes went by, and another delivery of moose soup arrived. This was almost too much, because I was only going to be in the village for a few days when Dominic Beans, a ninth grader, brought not only moose soup and bread but a salad as well.

This was more food than I knew what to do with, so I asked Dominic if he'd bring it back to his mother, thank her, and tell her to save it for another time.

Why all this food? To no surprise of mine, after Abe had called me he got on the CB and "announced" to the village that "Father hadn't eaten since he got in."

There is one unwritten rule in the villages that never goes unheeded: every guest is to be fed, even if it means going a little hungry yourself. The elders speak with pride of how their village feeds guests at the times of potlatch or other celebrations.

So what did I learn from this "slice-of-life?" If you're hungry, people will feed you, if you let them know. If you're too embarrassed to ask, you might be surprised, like I was, by the largess of the people when they find out you are hungry. ✝

The most consistent experience I have had in my journey is the kind of support and consolation I have had in going for direction. ***John V. Murphy, S.J.***

What Happens in Direction?
John V. Murphy, S.J.

I was distracted, down, and feeling very much alone. I had been neglecting my prayer—too busy, too pressured, and too depressed. I was feeling anxious about everything going on in my life. Classic desolation.

It was quite difficult to go for direction with these feelings of weakness and discouragement. I thought I should just "gut it out" and wait till the feelings passed and come to my friend with more positive feelings. On the other hand I felt drawn to meeting him, whatever my spiritual condition, by the memories of past visits. No matter what kind of a mess I had fallen into I had always left our sessions at peace.

The most consistent experience I have had in my journey is the kind of support and consolation I have had in going for direction. Sometimes there is not much joy in the Eucharist. Sometimes prayer is a bitch. Sometimes books of spiritual reading are a bore. But spiritual direction and the Word of God in Scripture are two unfailing sources of inspiration for me. "Bible roulette," praying to the Spirit and then opening Scripture at random, and talking to my director—I can always count on these gifts as nurturing my spirit.

What happens in direction? First, there is presence or, to paraphrase from the Gospel, "where two or three are gathered in my name." Jesus comes to me as he did on the way to Emmaus and consoles with his reminders of what he has said to his own on past occasions. Second is faith. Conversing together with another person who loves Jesus brings a renewed vividness to one's faith. This is true even when one, or particularly, when one is in desolation. Finally, there is love. "Love one another as I have loved you" is especially what I sense when receiving direction.

In a book review of a biography of Martin Luther King, Jr., in the *New Yorker* of April 6, 1987, the writer quotes a very hopeful message from the late civil rights leader about God's mercy: "God does not judge us by the separate incidents or the separate mistakes that we make, but by the total bent of our lives." And he goes on, "I want you to know this morning that I am a sinner like all of God's children, but I want to be a good man, and I want to hear a voice saying to me one day, 'I take you in and I bless you because you tried. It was well that it was within thy heart.'"

This fundamental goodness in my heart is what is affirmed by my director when he listens to me pouring out my little tale of troubles. By the end of the visit I am saying again, "Lord, it's good for me to be here." ✟

But in my deepest dreams and fondest reveries, I always find my greatest happiness in the Society.
Frank Case, S.J.

Life in Chastity
Frank Case, S.J.

A life of chastity finds its deepest meaning for me in my experiences of family and community, in both its narrowest and broadest sense.

My brother Dick Case* and I enjoy visiting the home of our sister, Mary. We can take whatever time we want to talk with and play with her kids—even to the point of getting them all hyped up—and then kiss or hug everyone good-bye as we head back blissfully to our celibate life in community. She gets to strap them down in their beds and pull the house back in order for another day. Her husband is, of course, a part of all of this.

When we thanked her once for providing us with the "joys of family life" without its burdens, she replied, "Yeah, you guys, how were you so darned smart when you were only teenagers to choose the life you chose?" She went on to analyze the vowed life in a rather humorous but very poignant way. We have a kind of financial security for our old age that few lay people have, although we certainly do not live in opulence. Our missioning in obedience generally involves at least a sensitivity to the individual's talents, desires, and needs (Mary would say we seem able to manipulate our superiors). And, as she put it, after a few kids the level of genital intimacy of a married couple isn't much greater than that of a faithful celibate.

While she put her remark about the life of religious chastity in terms of genital expression of intimacy, she was also implying, I believe, that we religious have much of the intimate love and support in our communities that married people enjoy in their family life. I have to say that this has certainly been true in my own case.

Besides this wonderful insight about community, Mary taught me, years earlier, something else about community life. She is now in her second marriage—a very happy one. But she was happily married to her first husband, when he died in an unfortunate auto accident. They had been married about five years at the time. We were talking shortly after the accident, and she said that one of the things that really griped her about her husband's death was the fact that they had worked so hard to make their marriage a really happy and good one, and now all that effort seemed to be for nothing. I thought, later on, that I have had to work at community life, at building or deepening the wonderful sense of rightness and love that I feel for the brethren and for the Society. Somewhere in the midst of that sense of rightness and love, my gift of a chaste life has its deepest mysterious meaning for me.

I told someone, when I started thinking about this topic several weeks ago, that I almost take my chastity for granted. Sure, I can be "tempted" or attracted to a lovely lass or lady. I have close women friends. But in my deepest dreams and fondest reveries, I always find my greatest happiness in the Society. I cannot imagine myself happy in any other sort of life. Like the elderly couple who can sit by the hour in unexpressed love for each other, I guess my love for the brethren and for the Society goes often unexpressed—and in that sense I take my chastity for granted—but it is nonetheless deep and oh so graced. God is very good to me. ✞

When I begin to doubt myself and ask myself if I am doing anything at all for the poor, I look at the people in my homes. **George Dumais, S.J.**

What Seems So Little So Very Big
George Dumais, S.J.

Last week I showed a movie to my freshman religion class. It was about a young Peace Corps volunteer who had adopted a little South American boy, or better, he had been adopted by the four-year-old boy. The movie showed what he was able to do for that child when he stopped theorizing or trying to give him and his people his expertise and just lived and shared this kid's life and the life of the community. Then he became loved, and then he had love to give them. While watching the film, I shed tears that my freshmen, those who noticed, could not understand.
I couldn't understand either until I reflected upon this incident.

Why the tears? The film was sad and it touched my heart-strings, but more than that, it struck a chord in my innermost being that made me realize how very little I am doing for the poor and how poor I am. It would be wonderful to be able to do more, always more.

And yet, hours, days, weeks, and months are too short and too few. Energy is limited. What is poverty? The temptation is to try to meet the needs of more and more handicapped persons, extending oneself without the time to nourish one's inner being. That is poverty!

And for the people at the residence that I run for mentally and emotionally disabled adults? What is poverty for them here in Missoula? They live in beautiful homes, with beautiful things surrounding them and with all the beauties that are Missoula's to give. They eat well and dress well and have a recreational and social life that most so-called normal people would envy. They are mainstreamed into the flow of real life. And yet they continue to be different. They are stared at when they go out. They are harassed and have water balloons and other objects thrown at them as they go from point *a* to point *b*. They are jeered at and called names. No one seems to understand them, and no one really seems to want to understand. Much can be done to help mainstream them, but they continue to be treated differently. This is poverty! No matter how much one does to assist them to "mainstream" into "real life," their situation continues to be misunderstood.

And so my people's poverty is great. Mine is great. No matter what I do, I cannot change people's attitudes towards the gents and ladies in my homes. I keep wanting to do more for them and others. I must check myself so that I don't say yes to yet another committee, another board created to meet more needs of the poor, the abused and neglected kids, and, the most recent arrivals, the Hmongs, Asian refugees whom I try to help assimilate into American culture. So much to do!

When I begin to doubt myself and ask myself if I am doing anything at all for the poor, I look at the people in my homes and, more particularly, I take a look at Jim's and Bill's lives. Jim spent twenty years in a state institution. Bill spent thirteen horrible years there. Both suffered immeasurably. We have lived together now for the past thirteen years, and I look at them and see new life. I see new beginnings for them. I was instrumental in creating for them a consistent, structured home, where they felt secure enough to get rid of the "craziness," where they could begin to build their self-esteem, and where they could learn new social and self-help skills. Jim is so successful at living life in the "real world" that he has held a job, the same one, for the past eleven years. He even pays taxes. Bill has done such a good job with his life that with just a little supervision he is almost capable of operating our home. These are the accomplishments of the "little ones," to borrow the phrase that the French-Canadian humanitarian Jean Vanier used to describe the poor. That brings blessings into my life and makes what seems so little so very big. ✝

71

No one takes the place of the Holy Spirit in spiritual direction; the Holy Spirit takes its own place. **John Navone, S.J.**

Jesus' Way of Spiritual Direction
John Navone, S.J.

After a number of years in the Society, some Jesuits profit from
a spiritual father for their spiritual direction; others, from
a spiritual brother. I have found most profit from the spiritual
brothers whose longstanding friendship in the Society has given
me a knowledge of myself that endows my conversation feed-
back with credibility. Our spontaneous "small talk" often
amounts to an informal spiritual direction in working our way
through everyday problems. Such Jesuit friends or spiritual
brothers are indispensable for an authentically Jesuit life.

I believe that joy is a hallmark of true spiritual direction. We
enjoy our spiritual brothers and friends with that joy, which is
the fruit of the Holy Spirit that we share. The spiritual brothers
who illuminate my Jesuit life have the quality of evoking gladness
and gratitude. We are glad to see them and grateful for their
companionship. We experience the joy-giving Spirit in their
friendships as God's gift for us. We encourage and enlighten one
another as spiritual brothers in that Spirit who is ultimately the
only true Spiritual Director. No one takes the place of the Holy
Spirit in spiritual direction; the Holy Spirit takes its own place.

I have not so much experienced its direction through formal
appointments with a spiritual director as in spontaneous conversations with Jesuit friends. Cardinal Carlo Martini, S.J., on that
score, once remarked in a lecture that conversation was Jesus'
ordinary or privileged way of spiritual direction. If faith implies
seeing the extraordinary, I believe that it is operative in our sense
of the spiritual good that we derive faith from our ordinary
conversations with good Jesuit friends. I believe that the Holy
Spirit takes and makes its place as Spiritual Director in the
authentic Jesuit friendships with our spiritual brothers. Through
the gift of his Spirit, Jesus continues to converse with us in the
conversation of our spiritual brothers, surprising us with how
much good there can be in "small talk." ✝

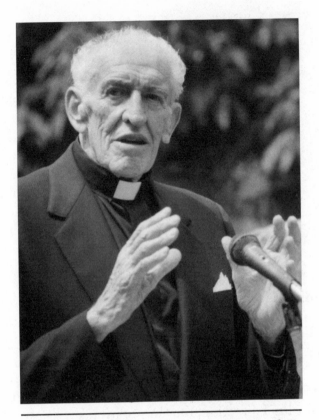

Omnia Ad Majorem Dei Gloriam—this is the shibboleth that has become a focal part of my Jesuit life. It is the root of Jesuit motivation. **Arthur L. Dussault, S.J.**

A Constant Golden Thread
Arthur L. Dussault, S.J.

In 1963, the Bozarth Chapel, dedicated to the Blessed Trinity, was erected as part of the new Jesuit house residence at Gonzaga University. A committee was appointed, of which I was a member, to offer a design for the reredos behind the altar, a devotional but spectacular mosaic, bordered by Italian marble and done in modern Byzantine style, that was made in West Germany.

The twenty-foot-high illuminated mosaic features the triumphal Christ seated on a throne holding a large cross in his left hand while rays from a triangle above, depicting God through the Paraclete, descend in a living flame of red, indicating the love of God through the Holy Spirit upon his Son, Christ Jesus.

Christ hands to the kneeling Saint Ignatius a folded banner where one can observe in the center circle the Jesuit monogram, I.H.S. The Society of Jesus is represented by four Jesuit saints: St. Robert Bellarmine, cardinal and educator; St. Ignatius Loyola, founder of the Society of Jesus; St. Francis Xavier, missionary apostle; and St. Aloysius Gonzaga, patron of youth and manifesting interested approval. The mosaic confirms the Ignatian vision that "they (Pope Paul III, the Church) would be propitious to him in Rome the next day."

Below this impressive mosaic is written on the bottom line: *Omnia Ad Majorem Dei Gloriam* —*A.M.D.G.* ("Everything for the greater glory of God"). This is the shibboleth that has become a focal part of my Jesuit life. It is the root of Jesuit motivation.

The Jesuits at Gonzaga High School encouraged us to use A.M.D.G. on all our assignment papers and correspondence. Spending eight years (1920–1928) with the Jesuits—two years at Gonzaga High School, four years at Gonzaga University, two years coaching sports and teaching at Gonzaga High School— before entering the Jesuit Order gave a special significance to A.M.D.G.

Since joining the Society of Jesus in 1928, I have found A.M.D.G. to be a constant golden thread that has held a slightly delayed vocation together, propounding the Spiritual Exercises of Ignatius Loyola through frequent exhortations, studies, triduums, and annual eight-day retreats in addition to three thirty-day retreats. It was the *magis* that challenged the Jesuit.

This aid to prayer life was amusingly jolted by one attorney, Joe Albi, a famed Gonzaga A.B. graduate of 1911, when he was the featured speaker at an alumni homecoming banquet I attended in the 1940s. A wit—who was also the perennial president of Spokane's famed and zany Athletic Round Table—he was wont to tease the Jesuits, which he did that evening by giving his interpretation of A.M.D.G. He insisted it meant "All the More Dough for Gonzaga." For me, my vocation, my educational apostolate, that wasn't too far off.

We who live at Jesuit House in Spokane are perennially blessed. This devotional reminder in its chapel, emblazoned on an inspiring mosaic, is a constant and spiritual encouragement, a pearl of great price, just for the prayer. ♱

Through collaborative work with lay teachers in crucial areas of faith and justice today, I have found that a university with its one thousand graduates a year is an endless field of ministry. **David Leigh, S.J.**

To Follow Not a Pious Image of Jesus
David Leigh, S.J.

I look out at a new class of twenty-five college freshmen. They struggle to grasp the point of Othello and gradually come to admit their own experiences with love and possessiveness and violence. They come to admire the genius of Shakespeare's language. They get excited at seeing Laurence Olivier bring Othello alive on screen or quoting from "Inversnaid" by the nineteenth-century English poet Gerard Manley Hopkins, "For Christ plays in ten thousand places/Lovely in limbs, and lovely in eyes not his. . . . through the features of men's faces."

These words strike me as I reflect on the ministry of teaching literature. From the Principle and Foundation, with its stress on how all things relate to our central drive for God, to the Contemplation, with its vision of all things as gifts within which God exists, labors, and loves us, I find the Spiritual Exercises provide the widest context for a Jesuit teacher. If God is creator, sustainer, and laborer in all gifts, he must be most present in human co-creations of literature. The challenge for me is to help students "find God in all things." This central dynamism of the creative loving Lord is perhaps why the Church and Society have, from the time of Ignatius to the Thirty-third General Congregation, affirmed the apostolate of teaching and research.

More personally, I have found great consolation in the Call of the King to work with him to bring all peoples to the Kingdom of God, a kingdom of peace and of freedom. In specifying this call, I have experienced God working through my vocation to the Society and to the priesthood but also through my talents for thinking, writing, and teaching. Affirmed by the Society and the Church, these talents are especially crucial for helping students who are at the decision-making center of their lives—the ages of sixteen to twenty-five. In those years, most students come alive intellectually, make their fundamental moral options, and undergo their first adult religious challenges. To work with Christ in a dorm, a classroom, a campus is to work with him at the crossroads of young Christian lives at the edge of the Kingdom.

Finally, I have experienced the Two Standards to be the most challenging part of the Exercises. To follow not a pious image of Jesus but the Christ who chose to be poor, humble, and suffering out of love for us is the key challenge of all Jesuits. This means that my work as a teacher must be to live closely with the spiritually, and sometimes economically, poor, with students strung out in dorms or classrooms, and with students in despair about the meaning of their lives. As a teacher, I go into others' lives armed not with the power of force but with the power of the search for beauty and truth. I must empty myself to bring others' minds and hearts to life. Through collaborative work with lay teachers in crucial areas of faith and justice today, I have found that a university with its one thousand graduates a year is an endless field of ministry. As a Jesuit I have struggled to promote a liberating education for justice and service—through a solid core curriculum, through international and peace studies, through students' activities, and through campus ministry—all of which, I trust, bring students closer to the standard of Christ. ✟

In prayer it is the Lord who helps me to attend to this voice without being controlled by it. **John Endres, S.J.**

Naming the Voices
John Endres, S.J.

In the last fifteen years I can recall seven spiritual directors.
While all have proven helpful to me, I'd like to describe three
singular breakthroughs, each while I was being directed by
a sister.

In my first year of theology at Weston School of Theology
in Cambridge, Massachusetts, I spent the first couple of months
in direction discussing my prayer and the transition to theology.
After several months I found the courage to ask the sister for her
help in an area of conflict in my life. I was upset by one of the
women at the school, whose manner around me and other
scholastics seemed overly familiar. I told my director that I'd
tried praying about it but without success. She then asked
if I could describe this woman's behavior to her as well as my
ideas about what it meant. After giving my version of what was
going on, she said, "You might be correct, but women may be
more different from you than you think, so you'll never know
until you ask her." I was terrified by her suggestion! But she went
on to suggest a prayerful way of preparing for such a conversation. She proposed that I imagine a setting where the woman
and I would converse in the presence of the Lord. During prayer
I could "rehearse" what I wanted to say and ask this woman—
in the presence of the Lord. So I tried this style of prayer—I really
learned what "repetitions" were all about—as I "repeated" the
prayer until I had the courage to speak to her in person. When
we finally spoke it was not a confrontation, for the Lord had
already taught me how to speak with her; it was actually a very
freeing and happy conversation for each of us. Since then I have
often used and recommended this method of prayer, rehearsing
before the Lord when preparing for a difficult conversation
or encounter.

During my graduate studies at Vanderbilt I got very discour-
aged about my daily prayer patterns. I thought I should be able
to pray as long and as well as in my earlier years of formation.
When I prayed less, I'd get upset, and then a pattern of disap-
pointment would set in, and things would just get worse.

My director helped me to examine my expectations and to experiment with a shorter time devoted to prayer. With her help I eventually settled on a half hour every morning, sometimes even a bit longer. What she helped me do was to find God in my daily life instead of fulfilling expectations, either mine or others. As I look back now, I remember proceeding in this way when directing others, but I needed a good director to get there myself.

Finally, since I've been teaching at the Jesuit School of Theology at Berkeley I've noticed some subtle patterns of self-pity, jealousy, and competition. One day I was discussing this with my spiritual director, and I mentioned that it often feels like there's a little, inner voice in me that goads me on to these feelings. She simply asked me if I could "name" that voice— she'd heard some other people talk this way, and some named their voices things like "Boy Wonder" and "Nobody Loves Me." Suddenly I was able to give my voice a name, and we both had a good laugh. But from then on I was able to address that voice by name when it got too loud and have even learned to converse with it in God's presence, during prayer. I've learned that my voice has some good things to say to me, but that it greatly exaggerates its significance and urgency. In prayer it is the Lord who helps me to attend to this voice without being controlled by it. If I were to look at this dynamic now in Ignatian terms, I'd simply say that the evil spirit speaks very wisely, since it knows my weaknesses and knows how to speak from them in order to confuse and discourage me. "Naming" that voice, like describing inner experiences, gives a director and myself a much better chance of distinguishing God's voice during daily life and reflection. ✞

*Not only does God work in ordinary
events, but the ordinary milieu of grace
is the natural and ordinary life that
we experience.* **Paul Fitterer, S.J.**

Some Sense of the Holy
Paul Fitterer, S.J.

My vocation illuminates a principle that I have tried to keep a part of my life ever since I experienced and responded to a call that, to me, was beyond my understanding. The principle: Not only does God work in ordinary events, but the ordinary milieu of grace is the natural and ordinary life that we experience. My problem is that too rarely are my eyes open enough to see that. The conviction that I was called to the Jesuits was one of those ordinary moments when even in my blindness I was compelled in some way to see God and hear God's call.

From very early in life, I had some sense of the holy. I longed for times that I could be alone, either in the hills around my home or in the church that was a part of my childhood. I felt some sense that God was in all that and that perhaps he wanted me to be a priest. Who can say how much of that is God or the familial environment that nurtured me or the idealistic times that followed closely upon the end of the Second World War. At any rate, I felt that "sense." But nothing really fanned that spark into life. Most of my education was in public schools. I had no real contact with the parish, although the parish priests were good, kind men. I had a cousin who was a Jesuit and naturally my thoughts, when I thought of priesthood, turned to being a Jesuit who taught.

It wasn't until I left the small pond of Ellensburg High School in Ellensburg, Washington, and moved to the big ocean of the University of Notre Dame that I experienced a crisis of loneliness and meaninglessness that again moved the question of vocation into consciousness. On a bleak autumn afternoon I remember going to confession and talking to the confessor. This wise, old gentleman, whose name I do not remember, discussed my loneliness and my sense of loss in finding some sort of direction for my life. He suggested that I take a vocational aptitude test and left the confessional with me to go to the counseling department to do just that.

I took the test and, when I went back for an evaluation, one of the occupations that was suggested by my profile was the vocation of priest. I remember being overwhelmed with a great sense of peace, that this was what I was to do with my life. I left the office, still bathed in that sense, that glow of peace, and spent the afternoon and evening in the chapel of my dorm. Since that time I have not had a sense of consolation that was as strong as those feelings. I knew nothing of the rules for discernment of spirit, but I knew that the sense was from God, and I must act on it. I did so that fall by entering Sheridan.

I do not know how that grace was confirmed. I do know that I developed a simple rule of thumb for myself: Were I to leave the Society and choose something else I would need to have as strong a sense of peace and consolation about that decision as I had about my decision to become a Jesuit. Certainly it was the memory of that event that got me through those difficult, seemingly absurd years of Jesuit training in the fifties, and it still stays in my mind as I try to chart my course through the troubled waters of the Roman Catholic Church of the 1980s and beyond. I also know that from this "natural" experience a context was provided for God to work and to call. The theology of the German theologian Karl Rahner is most reflective of my own: The depth part of human experience is where God is revealed. ✟

*Their encouragement, their great delight
when I began to recover my pep and
energy, their love and affection for me
as Bill LeRoux are manifestations of
community support that I shall always
love and cherish in the Jesuit
community of Seattle University.*
Bill LeRoux, S.J.

For Twenty-seven Uninterrupted Years
Bill LeRoux, S.J.

It is not often in the life of a Jesuit that he lives in the same community for twenty-seven uninterrupted years. I came to Seattle University a young priest to begin teaching theology, and now as one of the older Jesuits, I spend my days working in university relations. This means I have a great deal of contact with our alumni, and I try to raise some much needed money for the Campaign for Seattle University.

One of my greatest experiences of genuine community support over the years was in 1977. I was appointed acting dean of the College of Arts and Sciences in the spring of that year and later became a candidate for the position of dean. In March of 1978, Father William Sullivan selected me as the dean. Well do I remember when Bill Sullivan announced to the community during the social hour that he had asked me to accept the position, and I had agreed to serve as dean. The community, almost to a man, responded with such enthusiasm and approval. They were happy to have a Jesuit in that office, and I was proud to be the dean of the College of Arts and Sciences. I loved being dean, and I did my very best to lead the college and to promote the vital importance of liberal learning in Jesuit education.

During my years as dean, I always experienced the great support of the Jesuit community. They knew I was honest and straightforward in dealing with them and with their lay colleagues. There were no hidden agendas.

When I resigned as dean to begin a new career in university relations, the Jesuit faculty members were genuinely sorry to see me leave but were equally supportive of my new position.

In December, January, and early February of 1989, I experienced a very bleak time due to ill health and other complications. The Jesuits were so concerned that I was not my old self. Their encouragement, their great delight when I began to recover my pep and energy, their love and affection for me as Bill LeRoux are manifestations of community support that I shall always love and cherish in the Jesuit community of Seattle University. ✞

Mike listened well. His spirituality was simple and faith-filled. He got me out of my head and into my heart.
Jerry Chapdelaine, S.J.

Growing in the Lord
Jerry Chapdelaine, S.J.

I can honestly say that spiritual direction on a consistent basis
has affected my life. I have had several spiritual directors in my
years in the Society, three of whom I would like to single out.

In my years at St. Michael's, the philosophy school in Spokane
(commonly referred to as "the Mount") and regency at Gonzaga
Preparatory, I met regularly with Tim O'Leary. He was living in
DeSmet Hall at the time and teaching chemistry. He had the
reputation of being a very tough teacher but as a spiritual director he was sensitive, kind, understanding, and caring. His holiness touched me. Tim was quite directive. Relationship with
God was top priority. He made me accountable mostly with the
examen (awareness examen). Each time I visited him he asked
if I was faithful to my examen. He emphasized two things: prayer
for light and prayer of thanksgiving. He wanted to make sure
I was growing in the Lord.

In theology I met Father Joe Wall. He taught dogmatic theology and was very influential in my life not only as a teacher but
as a spiritual director. His approach was semidirective. I found
Joe to be an excellent listener who never wasted words. What
I remember most about him in direction was teaching prayer
on my feelings of the moment. I remember him many times
telling me to put away the Bible and give my feelings to the
Lord—loneliness, insecurity, hurt, lack of confidence, and doubt.
He had me use the scene of present feeling or situation for a first
prelude in prayer. Joe Wall really knew the Spiritual Exercises.
His whole approach was Ignatian.

Mike McHugh* was another person who directed me. His
method was indirect. I first started with Mike when he was at
St. Ignatius, and I was at the retreat house in Portland. He listened well. His spirituality was simple and faith-filled. He got
me out of my head and into my heart. Mike helped me develop
a deep appreciation of the Eucharist and reconciliation. His
direction in prayer always pointed toward the Mass and forgiveness. His direction was attractive, because it was simple and
uncomplicated. Faith was the bottom line.

I remember one time L. Pat Carroll*, Mike, and myself had finished making a "Better World Retreat" in Michigan. On our return trip the plane encountered some turbulence and Mike expressed this wish: "I hope the plane crashes so I can be with Jesus forever." L. Pat and I looked at each other in silence. ✞

*I was learning that if one can't experience love on a
human level, it is pretty hard to expect it with God.
Fred Mercy, S.J.*

Real Longings
Fred Mercy, S.J.

My views on celibacy cannot be discussed without including
women. So, I'll talk about both women and celibacy because
they are so closely related for me.

The story of my vocation is tied into life in general. I came to
God very early in life and more as an escape than love. I had
a sleep disorder called narcolepsy and could not function at all,
so I chose God as an escape rather than the more "normal" ones:
alcohol, drugs, and sex. I could, literally, not stay awake. I was
failing in school, because I couldn't stay awake in class,
I couldn't stay awake to read, and I even was known for sleeping
on the football field. My alert time was so limited that I had
to choose very carefully what, to me, were important things
in my life.

Unfortunately, women were not high on my list of important
items, so I eliminated them early in my decision-making process.
This, of course, was reinforced by my educational path. I attended all-male schools—grade school and high school. Only
when in college did I encounter women. Yet I still managed, in
all those years, to have very little to do with the opposite sex.
Only when I began to get some real control over my sleeping,
which happened in the Society, did I begin to deal with them.
In all this I can say, easily, that chastity, as a vow or a way of life,
was no problem at all. For me, it was the easiest of the three vows
in the Society. I simply ignored the other half of the human race.

In my late thirties I began to bring order and control into
my life, and it was then that I began to recognize my sisters.
It happened in my job as director of the Matt Talbot Center,
a sixty-bed dormitory hotel on Portland's skid row.

It was there that I noticed the young Jesuit Volunteers, who
usually happened to be women, and that I was "stuck" with
them. Finally, I had to begin to deal with women.

It was at that time that I was talking with my spiritual director
who used to ask me, "How are you getting along with your sisters?" I would respond, "Great!" and didn't even know I really
was not. I would add, "What's that got to do with Jesus?" "If you

don't love your sisters whom you do see," he challenged, "how can you love God whom you can't see?" He taught me a very important spiritual lesson. Life up to then had been safe, for I protected myself from affection or sexual feelings, and never experienced love by never getting involved. I was learning that if one can't experience love on a human level, it is pretty hard to expect it with God. I had to begin from scratch. I had to go through the social-sexual stages of development that others usually go through at an earlier age.

There is another factor in this whole scenario. I qualify for A.C.O.A. (Adult Children of Alcoholics). One characteristic of this group is that we bury our feelings. I had ignored women and my feelings for them for years, but the Lord was telling me that if I wanted to love him I had better learn to love my sisters. This would involve changing my thought patterns, because the decisions I had made as a kid were now holding me back. I discovered that chastity does not mean isolation. So now I needed to learn how to love, how to be vulnerable, how to need others, and how to feel. I had buried my sexual feelings all those years.

My journey since my new beginning has been fraught with many episodes that might be considered scandalous by some and even close to breaking my vow, but I have always known that God is protecting me. The women who have come into my life in these years have been teaching me about feelings, about love, about themselves, and about me. They have brought me to a place where my vow is now tough and difficult, because I have learned what is involved. I feel now, at fifty-seven, that I could get married, possibly even enjoy it, and not be afraid of a relationship. So this brings us back to that ongoing question every religious asks at one time or another, "Why stay? Why keep the vow of chastity?"

My whole journey, I hope, is based on my ultimate goal: to love God with my whole heart, soul, and being. There are many reasons for taking and keeping the vow of chastity, but what keeps me in the Society is my desire to return to Jesus and my relationship with him. If the relationship is good and active then it's his presence in my life that keeps me faithful to prayer, which is, to me, what good communications are to a married couple. Again, if this is good, it keeps me from seeking relationships outside my initial commitment. I have found God to be faithful to me in this area even though I am more susceptible to heartache than before and much more aware of what I have chosen to give up.

Currently, I am getting along great with women (at least I think so). I could never have even imagined this ten years ago. I now have real longings that could undermine my vow, but what I used to count as "temptations" are healthy sexual responses to the presence of women. Because of these sexual feelings I now know that my commitment demands a price.

At the same time, I am also growing in the love of Jesus. I feel he will see me through painful moments and guide me in my relationships with women. ✝

In my years in Alaska my eyes have been opened to the wealth that the native people possess and the impoverishment that I bring to my ministry among them.
Dick Case, S.J.

Learning to See
Dick Case, S.J.

In the summer of 1970, Jack Murphy, the dean of studies, sent me to Alaska to learn about the missions. At first I found a position with Upward Bound at the University of Alaska as a tutor-counselor for Native American high school students. Even Fairbanks, with its thirty thousand people, seemed a bit isolated and wild. Just over the hills, in any direction, was open tundra with no roads and no population. Quite frankly, the vastness of the state frightened me a little.

After several weeks in Fairbanks, I joined Jim Sebesta, a preeminent Jesuit pilot, on a flight to some of the bush mission sights. After a few days with him traveling through truly remote parts of Alaska, I began a love affair with the state and its people. The next summer I spent with Bill Dibb, another co-worker, learning more about the way people live and work in territory covered by the Fairbanks diocese. After those two summers, my whole direction in the Society turned toward serving the people of Alaska. In 1976, the provincial assigned me to the Alaska superior for an indefinite period.

Living and working among the Yupik people of western Alaska has taught me to see what was at first obscure. To the casual observer, the native people of western Alaska may seem deprived of the necessities of life. They appear to be materially impoverished. It has become apparent to me that anyone who lacks what I consider necessary to live is impoverished. In some cases the observation is correct. In many cases, however, the observation is clouded, because the values with which the observer judges the other people is itself impoverished. In my years in Alaska my eyes have been opened to the wealth that the native people possess and the impoverishment that I bring to my ministry among them.

When I first arrived in western Alaska, I experienced the land as empty and dangerous. The only places where I felt safe were in the villages and towns, where there were plenty of people and plenty of shelter. The tundra had no roads and no places to land in case of an emergency. There were no houses for shelter and no places to find food. It took a few years to learn that the natives of western Alaska had long lived on the land that I considered empty and dangerous. They knew how to find shelter and how to find food even in the emptiest looking area. One time while flying one of the deacons to Tununak, I watched his face as he looked at the tundra below us. His eyes looked with love upon a land that had given him and his family life for so long. There was no fear of the land that I experienced. Slowly, I came to realize that he did not think of the land as belonging to him but of himself as belonging to the land.

The best of native culture guides the people to live in harmony with a generous and life-giving creation. They do not think of themselves as capturing an animal or a fish. They think of the animals and fish as giving themselves to the community for life. The good hunter has a spirit in sympathy with the spirit of the animal. Thus the animal feels comfortable giving itself to the people in order to keep them alive. When a hunter kills a seal he pours a little fresh water into its mouth as a sign of respect and welcome. With our modern spirituality we might be tempted to see such a practice as superstitious and silly until we understand the background from which the practice arises.

It has become clearer to me that any attempt to improve the lives of people from another culture requires great sensitivity to the wealth they already possess. In order to help others we must first determine with them what it is that they lack for a full and worthwhile life. One thing that poor people lack in the face of a modern technological culture is the true power to make decisions that will improve their lives. Too often outsiders— people who are usually more outspoken and self-confident— set the goals for change in their lives. During my time with the native people of Alaska, I became more and more aware of a helplessness that I had never experienced before in my life. The poor are not the only ones who need to change. Our culture needs to submit itself to the test of the Gospel. Our culture needs to change. ✞

St. Ignatius said that with poverty comes insults and with insults humility and with humility all other virtues.
Thomas G. Williams, S.J.

With Humility, All Other Virtues
Thomas G. Williams, S.J.

A few semesters ago I was delivering the sacraments in Jamaica. Almost everyone on my list was poor, sick, old, and illiterate.

First on the list was an old man who was so poor he could only afford one name. Stover. He lived all alone on the top of a hill, out in the woods, sixty yards to the nearest house and one mile to the nearest road. Privacy. He would be sitting on the steps, and when I came into view he would recite from Isaiah, "How beautiful upon the mountains are the feet of him who brings glad tidings." He couldn't read, but somewhere along the line he had committed this to memory.

After Communion we would visit, and he would tell me how peaceful it was here. He had no electricity or running water. I noted that he cooked outside on an open fire. His shack, with its pit toilet very close, did not lead to covetousness. My smile and nod indicated that I heard him.

Mrs. Lavander Prescott would be waiting for me on her front porch in her old rocking chair. Though not a *Guinness Book* contender, Mrs. Prescott—who was somewhat on the heavy side—was no one's first choice for a trapeze partner. After the prescribed time, we visited. She once told me, "I've got the sugar and the pressure and the heart and they is afflicting me to my God." Sugar diabetes, high blood pressure, and heart trouble. How fortunate can you be to have those three body clerks reminding you to plan on an early check out? I smiled and nodded.

Next was Shakey Green. He had worked on electric power lines before the accident. After that, he could just show up and take at least a third in any jitterbug contest. His house was located on the side of a steep mud slide that made getting there a difficult feat. The house was easily the size of two piano boxes joined together. Since Shakey didn't own a piano, or much of anything else, there was plenty of room. He thought that the splendid location kept thieves and ruffians from dropping in and complicating his life. He was content with his lot in life and said so. I smiled and nodded.

Mrs. Adelia Washington lived in a very small home in the high crime area of Montego Bay. Nonresidents were not welcome unless they were doctors of medicine, nurses, nuns, or "pastors." If you were one of those four flavors, you wore a uniform to indicate your profession. I was always incredibly alert on my visits there (scared).

Mrs. Washington would close the shutters and door so we could have some privacy from the wide-eyed children who stared in to see what the "tall ripe father" was doing. After praying in silence, she would tell me that her early days had been hard, and it was only in the recent past that she was able to live in such peace and security. She was all sincerity. I smiled and nodded.

These were typical of the people on the list. They were poor. They were humble. They were at peace with their God. St. Ignatius said that with poverty comes insults and with insults humility and with humility all other virtues.

I never told them this, but if I had I am sure that they, who were into the practice not the theory, would have looked at me, smiled, and nodded. ✝

During the months prior to making my decision to apply I also experienced moments of fear—I knew it was a big step. **Jake Morton, S.J.**

A Wonderful Thing Happened
Jake Morton, S.J.

The year I worked at the S & S Grocery in my home town of
Colfax, Washington, was a turning point for me. I was a junior
in high school. Until then I had wanted to be a veterinarian
or perhaps an electrician like my dad or perhaps—I wasn't
at all sure what I wanted. But Ray Nelson, owner and manager
of the service-oriented S & S, initiated me into the world of
helping people. One specialty of the store was home delivery.
People could phone in their orders, and we would deliver them.

I remember one of our customers—a middle-aged, single
woman who was blind. I would carry the bags into her kitchen
and place them on her table. Item by item, I would hand her each
thing, tell her what it was, and she would put it in her cupboard.
I was profoundly moved by this experience. At the end of that
year I still didn't know what I wanted to do with my life, but
I was absolutely certain that I wanted a life that focused on being
of service to people, especially the poor and the vulnerable.

During my freshman year at Gonzaga University I had enrolled
in premed, thinking that perhaps medicine would be a way of
living out my new ideal of service. But in my heart I was far from
sure. It was a year of searching and pondering. Two things happened that year that opened the door to the Jesuits. First, Jack
Leary, in the process of rescuing me from failing his philosophy
class, asked if I had ever considered the priesthood. I said
I hadn't. He encouraged me to give it some thought as a possibility for myself. I was in shock at his directness. I said, "Yes, I would
think about it." As I was leaving he mentioned the names of
several of my classmates who were entering the Society of Jesus
the following year. He encouraged me to talk with them.

Meeting these classmates was the second thing that put my
life in the direction of the Jesuits. I remember thinking that each
one was so unique, and yet they were all so ordinary, so real.
Jim McGloin*, Tom Provinsal, Kevin Clark, Joe Mark, and others.
And talk we did. Like them, I felt drawn to do something, to offer
myself, to help other people in some way. My prayer about this
was deep and peaceful and consoling. I was also attracted to the

"brotherhood" of the Jesuits; I liked their style, their common sense ways.

During the months prior to making my decision to apply I also experienced moments of fear—I knew it was a big step. I remember going out to a lake cabin with Joe Mark in the late fall. We talked late into the night around the fire. We spoke of our fears and our desires, and Joe paraphrased the lines of a Robert Frost poem that seemed to capture both: "The woods are lovely, dark and deep, and I have many promises to keep, and miles to go before I sleep."

During the novitiate I had one very disturbing crisis/confrontation experience. I went to see Frank Mueller, our novice master, and said, "Father, I'm beginning to think I've made a mistake!" I explained that I did not feel attracted to any of the Jesuit works I had seen. I couldn't see myself teaching, working in a big parish, or being a retreat master. I was beginning to panic. He listened very patiently and seemed to understand. His good advice was, "Give it time. Keep it in your prayer, and we'll also talk more about it. And remember, you haven't seen all the works of the Society yet." I was reassured, but still left with an empty feeling regarding the works I had seen.

And then a wonderful thing happened. Missionaries began to visit the novitiate from Zambia and Alaska. As they described their work, their people, the diversity of cultures and languages, I was filled with joy and longing. The native peoples of Alaska and the Northwest have been the focus of my Jesuit life ever since then. Thank you, Norm Donahue, Jake Spills, Paul O'Conner, and all the others, for sharing your vision of service with us. The native peoples first invited the Jesuits to the Northwest. And now they continue to invite us to collaborate with them in their vocation of becoming a truly indigenous Catholic Church. ✝

And yet it is the poor who call us to forgiveness and unity, and it is our own poverty that opens our hearts to God.
David Rothrock, S.J.

It Is the Poor Who Call Us
David Rothrock, S.J.

I am happy to have the opportunity to share my experiences with
the poor, because it has been my privilege over the greater part
of the past fifteen years as a chaplain with the L'Arche movement—a movement that welcomes all peoples to come together
in community—to live with brothers and sisters who are poor
and wounded in their intelligences and their bodies. They are
people who have suffered not only because of their own handi-
cap but also due to the rejection by others, sometimes by their
own families.

Richard was deaf and for that reason was placed in an institution for the mentally retarded at the age of eleven. Forty-five
years later he came to live with us and began a normal life in
a normal home. It was not that he was treated badly in the institution—to the contrary, the staff loved him. But living among
one thousand people and a staff who come and go three shifts
a day is hardly home. He never was taught to learn to read or
to use sign language, so communication with Richard was difficult. We would all jump into the car and head off somewhere
forgetting to inform Richard where we were going. So often
he had to trust us and hope that where he was being led was all
right and that he would come back. He also suffered because
he did not have the tools to express his inner feelings—especially
those of anger, hurt, sadness, and depression. He was a man of
frequent forgiveness and great kindness.

Richard made many friends in the neighborhood, at church,
and within the L'Arche community. He endeared himself to
others, especially children, in kindness and care. He was not
handicapped in his heart. Richard's arrival in our community
enabled him to give the gift of his person and have it received
by many. He enriched the lives of many people through his
friendship and showed to us all that the greatest gift of God—
love—is of the heart. He showed us that to receive that gift we
need humility—a poverty of spirit. Richard died last February
of an apparent heart attack. Richard is deeply missed in our
community and is prayed for and remembered as we would

remember any family member. I am especially grateful to Richard for he became a real brother and friend.

I first met Nancy a couple of years ago in a state institution for severely and profoundly handicapped children. Nancy was seventeen years old and had suffered severe nerve damage in a near drowning accident at the age of eight. Nancy is in a wheelchair and is dependent on others for most of her personal needs. She cannot speak, but she can hear. Nancy can feed herself and can write. Her smile conveys a quickness and a brightness that is hidden behind her disability and her slow movements. After a year of administrative hassle, we welcomed Nancy into our community. We especially wanted her to be with us because her parents were both dead, and there are no close family members. She has brought much joy into our community.

Nancy communicates through finger spelling, some sign language, a typewriter, and a "handi-voice," an electronic voice she manipulates through a keyboard. However, communication with her is very slow and requires patience and presence as she spells out each word. I found that I rarely had the patience to be with her. In the first few months of living with Nancy, I would kid her, laugh with her, help her, run around with her—all ways that I thought were creating a relationship with her. Then I realized I was kidding myself and missing her completely. I needed to stop, sit down, look her in the eyes, and be quiet, and wait so she could express herself and say what she wanted. I needed to learn to receive Nancy's gift and that required patience and presence. Nancy showed me that any relationship with God is much the same. I'm coming around and doing good things, but how important it is to stop, sit down, be quiet, and let God speak to me.

I am writing this in Madras, India, where I am visiting the L'Arche communities and giving retreats. These are little communities trying to live the Gospel of Jesus and the beatitudes by sharing one's life with the poor. They are so little and so hidden yet such a light of hope.

There is a line separating the rich and the poor, the powerful and the weak. That line runs through our world separating the rich countries from the poor countries. It runs through Central America where the rich are armed against the poor. That same line runs through our country, our cities, through our institutions, and our culture. It runs through our families and finally it runs through our own hearts. We always want to live out of the rich side of ourselves—where we are strong, capable, and in control. And we often hide behind our capacity and our strength.

And yet it is the poor who call us to forgiveness and unity, and it is our own poverty that opens our hearts to God. Poverty of spirit and humility are the essential condition of receiving the gift of God, which is love. So I am thankful to Richard and Nancy and many others for their precious gift of friendship and their constant reminder of the road to the Kingdom of God. They have a gift for the Church and the world that is a treasure and needs to be discovered. And so it is up to us to choose on which side of the line we want to live and on which side of the line we want to die. ✞

*My companions in the Lord have many
wide and varied talents and are selfless
in their commitment to the students and
parents we serve.*
Patrick M. Flannigan, S.J.

There Is a Bonding
Patrick M. Flannigan, S.J.

I look upon my role as minister at Jesuit High as being an
instrument in the Lord's work. I take the talents I have been
given and put those at the Lord's service in order to make our
living together harmonious by providing the necessities for
a common life and by helping to create an environment where
the Eucharist and the Spiritual Exercises nourish us to be alive
to one another and to the people we touch at school. My companions in the Lord have many wide and varied talents and
are selfless in their commitment to the students and parents
we serve.

I find my work as counselor very fulfilling through the environment that has been created by the efforts of the administration
and the campus ministry program. The Eucharist, the Spiritual
Exercises, and the Junior Encounter program have transformed
this school. These three have set us apart from the other
schools in Portland in community building—between students
and teachers, students and their families, and Jesuits and
our coworkers.

There is a bonding that began with my companions in the
Lord, and through the work of the Spirit, is now touching students, coworkers, and parents. This bonding is manifested in
the response of students who want to be Eucharistic ministers
or leaders in the retreat programs. It is witnessed in the coworkers who selflessly give of themselves beyond the school day.
It is revealed in the parents who volunteer because of what
they see going on within their sons. This blessed bond between
community and apostolate makes my commitment one of
thanksgiving to the Lord for my call to the Society and to
secondary education. ✝

It is clear to me that what I am doing is what I want to do because it is what the Spirit wants me to do.
William Hayes, S.J.

It Is Clear to Me
William Hayes, S.J.

Discernment is an essential ingredient of Ignatian spirituality.
Discernment for me took on a new light when on sabbatical
I took a course from Bernie Tyrrell* on the Holy Spirit. This
course opened my eyes to the Holy Spirit. Instead of being a
distant kissing cousin, the Spirit became a very intimate part
of my spiritual life.

St. Augustine said that the Holy Spirit is more intimate to you
than you are to yourself. Prayer, reflection, and understanding
about this statement made me realize more deeply that when
I get in touch with myself—my feelings, my fears, my joys, the
peace, the anxiety—it is really the Holy Spirit that I am in touch
with, and that is how I truly discern what the Lord is saying.

Through prayerful experience and through this intellectual
understanding of the working of the Spirit, it is clear to me that
my talents and my desires lie in educational administration on
the secondary level. And I am doing today exactly what I want
to do, because it is what the Holy Spirit wants me to do. I am
convinced of that.

Coming to this conclusion through discernment was not
quick and easy. It was somewhat painful and time-consuming,
but the end result was very clear and evident. In the process of
coming to a decision to be in administration at Jesuit High
School, a great amount of letting go had to take place. I had
to put myself in the hands of the Spirit, and let go of what I
could control.

In the process of discernment and letting go, it became
evident that to be involved in administration is necessary and
important to the Jesuit educational apostolate, that the experiences of my life have prepared me for this kind of work, that
I enjoy administration, that I can do it well, and that the opportunity to influence for good is extremely high.

Although I do not have personal contact with students the
way a teacher does, it is clear to me that my role of influencing
the students is still most important, because I am involved in
the decision about who the teacher in the classroom will be,

the quality, the capability, and the talent of the person. Even in fund-raising, I find a real sense of peace and calm, because it is the work of the Spirit in me.

In asking people for money I have found more often than not I become involved in personal conversations and often deeply spiritual conversations. I share the joy of the benefactors' appreciation of what Jesuit education is all about and why they are willing to share their treasure to support Jesuit education. This is a joy that the teacher in the classroom does not have in the same way one cannot see the forest for the trees.

I find educational administration and development work extremely meaningful for the reasons stated above as well as many other reasons, but most importantly because it is clear to me that what I am doing is what I want to do because it is what the Spirit wants me to do. And the more I can grasp and grapple with and understand the fact that the Holy Spirit is more intimate to me than I am to myself, the easier it becomes to truly get in touch with where the Lord is in my life and where I would like to be in my life. ✝

*As he lay in his hospital bed, I imagined that this bearded man was Jesus. **Roy Mann, S.J.***

Jesus' Hands and Feet

Roy Mann, S.J.

After graduating from the Catholic University of America,
I moved into Christ House, a health care project for the homeless
in inner-city Washington, D.C. Working as a full-time volunteer,
I remember my stay there as a time to meet Jesus in our homeless guests. Take Gerald McKenzie, for example. Gerald broke
his leg while jumping off a bridge in an attempt to commit
suicide. I still twinge when I think of the first time I saw Gerald's
leg exposed. Puss-filled and swollen, the indentation on his shin
looked like a crater. Without some kind of immediate medical
help, Gerald's leg may have needed amputation. At George
Washington Hospital, I found a leg specialist who agreed to
examine Gerald.

It took two buses to get across town to the doctor's office.
At the bus stop, Gerald fidgeted and twirled his brown beard
and then squatted down toward the pavement, picking up a half-
smoked cigarette. Waiting didn't agree with his schizophrenia.
Living off the street seemed like such a humiliation. It made me
feel Gerald's poverty. Eventually, we arrived at the hospital.
Nervous and on edge, Gerald hobbled into the doctor's office.
After a brief examination, the specialist set up a bone graft
operation that saved Gerald's leg.

More than some sort of do-gooder, I accompanied Gerald for
the sake of nurturing my love-relationship with Jesus. It was
a meditation. When I fixed my gaze on the gash in his leg,
I imagined Jesus' wounds. "God! Jesus' hands and feet must have
looked like that," I thought. And a poignant feeling overcame me.
I still remember visiting Gerald after the operation. All jittery,
he kept pestering me for a cigarette. So I went across the street
and got him a pack of Marlboro Lights. By the time I returned to
his room, Gerald had fallen asleep. As he lay in his hospital bed,
I imagined that this bearded man was Jesus. Then I whispered
a prayer, placed the smokes on his lap, and went on my way. ✝

We loved God with our whole heart, our whole mind, and our whole soul, and we were convinced he was calling us to prove that love by serving him and his cause in the Society of Jesus.
John Hurley, S.J.

The Support We Give and Receive
John Hurley, S.J.

When I was asked to reflect, publicly, upon my more than fifty years in the Society I did not suffer real or pseudo humility. I was glad to comply, because I honestly felt my story might prove helpful to some.

Fifty years ago young men entered the Society for the same reason they always had, and still do. We loved God with our whole heart, our whole mind, and our whole soul, and we were convinced he was calling us to prove that love by serving him and his cause in the Society of Jesus.

The most profound and lasting impression made upon a Jesuit novice is through the Thirty-day Retreat, the Spiritual Exercises. In the most literal sense the retreat, sometimes called the Long Retreat, is the same for every Jesuit novice. In each one's personal experience, however, certain elements of the Exercises enter more deeply than others.

Looking back now upon my first retreat, and all subsequent ones, I find that two points in the Exercises have entered most deeply into my consciousness and into the shaping of my Jesuit life. The initial point is the First Principle and Foundation. God is absolutely my first beginning; he is absolutely my final end. Out of infinite love he created me in his likeness, and that living, ever questing image and likeness can never be whole or happy till like meets like, till the likeness returns fully to its model, the Supreme Reality whence it came.

The second element of the Exercises that has been most influential in my life is, of course, an aspect of the central point of the Exercises, my personal relation to Jesus Christ. The aspect I refer to is the indwelling of Our Lord within my being. "I am the Vine, you are the branches." "That you may be one in me as I am one in the Father." And I love that prayer at the Offertory: "Through the Mystery of this water and wine may we become sharers in the Divinity of Jesus Christ who humbled Himself to share in our humanity." The implications of all this for devout Christians, Jesuits, and priests need no pointers for this readership.

At the same time, I must say something quickly to bring down the raised eyebrows of my contemporaries. I am not, I am sorry to say, a saint. The points of the Exercises that most influenced me have not worked that miracle, yet. But there is a miracle they have helped me to recognize. It is this: Whenever my life and actions bring someone, including me, closer to the Lord, that's Jesus and I together. All other times it's just old Padre John, all by myself.

Let's move on to another major influence I have experienced in the Society. Most Jesuits, I am sure, would agree with me that the support we give and receive through our friendship in the Society is a major part of the hundred-fold Our Lord promised to those who follow him. Recalling my struggles through the novitiate, the juniorate, the philosophy, the regency, the theology, and the tertianship, I can see how it would all have been impossible without the daily sustaining encouragement of my fellow Jesuits.

All former problems seemed petty compared to the one that fell heavily upon me following ordination and tertianship— a simple problem but monumental in its implications. Given so little talent, what sort of contribution could I ever make to fulfill the hopes the Church reposed in its Jesuits?

Then came the day I'll never forget. Father Frank Corkery called me over to his office. He was rector-president of Gonzaga University, and I was assistant principal of Gonzaga Preparatory. I remember he was shaving as I entered his private room, and he continued shaving as he talked. "Sit down, Father John. We have a problem. We are falling behind in our pledges for the new high school. Someone told me that you might be a good man to take care of the problem." I didn't really want the job. I had never asked anyone for money, but I took the job anyway. The year was 1953.

I still have that job.

Through the intervening years I have received many blessings—God's Providence through my superiors, and, to my surprise, I found a work I could do to help me, help my fellow Jesuits, and help our coworkers to spread the Kingdom of God. Oh, yes, there have been down days. Trying to extract money from people, even for the greatest of causes, is not something that of itself makes one's heart swell with pride or carries one trippingly through the days. But when I felt the "blahs" engulfing me I would say to myself, "What if they had given you a class in Greek or math to teach? You would have failed. The job they gave you, you can do. Do it." My courage would return and I could go back to work happy that I was doing something that helped the Church, the Oregon province, and Gonzaga Preparatory.

That happiness is strong within me in my daily Mass. There I give profound thanks to the Lord who in his infinite kindness has made me an instrument to help benefactors and beneficiaries of Gonzaga Prep, to promote his great honor and glory. ✝

*I value the little child within me—
my openness, my spontaneity, and
my honesty.* **Mark McGregor, S.J.**

He's On to Something
Mark McGregor, S.J.

Knitted *Sesame Street* characters smile from their places on the
wall, a huge jar sits half-filled with M & M's, and a comfy recliner
give character to my spiritual director's office—our usual meeting place. I laugh as I say this, but the room could be mistaken
for that of a child psychologist's office. Often enough I feel like
a little kid when I leave from the twice-a-month visit with Father
B., because I seem to hear and relearn a few simple lessons over
and over. Of course the variables change and the particulars
vary, but some basic issues and lessons about myself and the
Lord surface.

I value the little child within me—my openness, my spontaneity, and my honesty. These are precisely the things that get lost
in my need to control, in falling into a stagnant rut, and in my
own deception. In spiritual direction I seem to return to these
themes again and again. Like one who has learned by rote,
I receive subtle messages that reinforce a truth often heard
before. With the help of my spiritual director I find myself beginning to pick up clues in the lesson of life through a gift in which
I believe Ignatius would most desire me to grow—the gift of
discernment. I could not discern nor help others discern if
somehow I did not entrust myself to a relationship wherein
I went back to fine tune or relearn what I often know so well
in my head yet recognize faintly.

The familiar phrase "What I hear you saying" or the question
"What goes on in your prayer when you talk with Jesus about
that?" are just as familiar to me as that jar of M & M's in Father
B.'s office. The conversation that spiritual direction engenders
often reveals the responses that are dormant within me but,
which I have been too busy, too lazy, or too afraid to let surface.

When speaking to my spiritual director last year something
that I found difficult to own up to was called to my attention.
I talked, he listened; he responded, then I listened.

"Oh, no, it's not that at all," I insisted.

Further probing brought more head wags and denials—
though I began to say to myself, "He's on to something."

My fingers dug into the arms of the chair. I looked up long enough to catch my director's glance. I was pegged, and I knew it!

"Yeah," I admitted with a smirk, "yeah, maybe you're right." Then I began to laugh very hard. I continued laughing, because I was so amused by the folly of trying to hide from what seemed so clear. My director laughed right with me.

After minutes of chuckling, I saw the laughter as a collapse of a few barriers that I had wanted to remove. My director was persistent and honest enough to point something out but gentle enough to let me remove my barriers.

New issues and circumstances will inevitably come into my life, bouncing me between consolation and desolation. But I see myself returning to a few sources of struggle and grace that will doubtlessly reappear in the guise of different faces throughout the years. In spiritual direction I have grown more attentive in discerning those faces. I expect that they will be as numerous as Father B.'s M & M's, but as long as Big Bird or Cookie Monster and those M & M's are there I figure I will always be learning their identity over and over.

Who knows? Maybe from it all we grow in learning to take care of and pray for one another more often. ♱

In their poverty there was holiness as well as wisdom. **J. Patrick Hurley, S.J.**

How Then Does One Evaluate?
J. Patrick Hurley, S.J.

In 1974, I was accepted into the Horizons for Justice program
and spent five weeks in the parish of St. Paul the Apostle,
a reevangelized Christian community in the suburban slums
of Managua, Nicaragua.

I thought I had done my homework for the experience by
reading Octavio Paz and Oscar Lewis on the Latin American
character and the subculture of poverty. I also read Ruben Dario
and Ernesto Cardenal, two of the most famous Nicaraguan
writers, both of them poets.

But I really wasn't well prepared, not at all. There is simply no
way to prepare from books, even those written by poets, for the
intensity of tropical heat and the violent afternoon torrents, for
the dust, or for what happens in a city where physical misery is
heaped atop an impossible pile of injustice and neglect. And yet
there is still much to celebrate: the giving and taking in marriage
and the miracle of birth. People still laugh and dance, and the
Church is still uniquely present evangelizing and identifying with
the poor and the oppressed.

According to the Horizons policy statement, I was supposed
to "experience something of the vulnerability of the poor and
powerless" during my five-week stay.

I experienced the vulnerability in the parish neighborhood
where there were more than sixty thousand people; where every
family has a watchdog because many were living in tents (the
earthquake had occurred eighteen months earlier), since it is not
easy to lock up a tent at night; where dogs were inoculated due
to a rabies epidemic; where malaria spread; and where there
is malnutrition, and a baby is buried every single day.

I experienced the powerlessness when I stood looking into
the casket of a young mother and then tried to speak my priest-
speech that was expected of me and so necessary in the dust
and confusion. Just a word from me to dispel the absurdity, and
I couldn't find it, could only stare dumb across the body into the
eyes of her husband and her mother.

I was also programmed "to come to understand some of the riches possessed by the poor and powerless."

I did come to understand, as I sat with the people and read and reflected on the Gospels with them. I wondered at their insights and their eloquence. I wondered, too, about my twenty-four years of formal education, about the thousands of books and periodicals I have read, about the luxury of quiet conversations and workshops and meetings, and about chats in our conference rooms and overstuffed chairs. I wondered about my presence with them, stumbling into their lives, spying in a way, but still half-blind and spiritually tongue-tied. In their poverty there was holiness as well as wisdom.

And how then does one evaluate novitiates and monastery gardens and annual retreats and spiritual directors and the wealth of the Church that is lavished on those of us who are not poor, not chaste, not obedient, often less patient, persevering, and kind, and sometimes even possessed of a cold reason that passes for faith and a hope that is sustained by economic indicators?

I understood their riches when at midnight, beneath my window, the young men of the parish sang a farewell *serenata* and next morning, as I boarded the jeep for town, they asked, "*Hermano Patricio, ¿nos vas a volver?*" and I had to reply, "No, I will never be able to come back." ✝

They know that there is always someone they can call on, even if it's in the middle of the night. **James E. Royce, S.J.**

Rich Are the Poor, in Spirit
James E. Royce, S.J.

I work with alcoholics. Many of them are poor, not because
the typical alcoholic is a desperate panhandler, but because
the disease of alcoholism has caused them to lose jobs and
financial resources that once made them doctors, lawyers,
bankers, plumbers, or priests. Research has shown that the
average alcoholic is above-average in intelligence and talent.

But they are rich spiritually. I am not talking about Matt
Talbot, the devout Irish alcoholic who some think should be
canonized. I mean the many men and women of all ages who
have risen from the hell of alcoholism through the beautiful
spiritual program of Alcoholics Anonymous.

Nearly forty years ago I had a guest speaker from Alcoholics
Anonymous in my alcoholism course at Seattle University who
said, "I'm glad I'm an alcoholic." I thought, "What? After all
the hell she's been through?" And then she went on to explain
very simply that if she had not been an alcoholic she would
never have joined Alcoholics Anonymous, and she would never
have discovered how much God loved her and how much she
loved God.

Alcoholics help one another. It is common for a group of A.A.
members to pitch in and move a poor person to another apartment or fix up their car. They know that there is always someone
they can call on, even if it's in the middle of the night. They
genuinely love one another, and I don't mean going to bed
with them (that's called the Thirteenth Step, and it's a "no-no"
in A.A.). Go to a regional meeting of Alcoholics Anonymous
and watch the hugging and happy greetings of welcome and
reacquaintance that goes on. Someone has said that in Alcoholics Anonymous we see the one modern instance of primitive
Christianity: "See how they love one another."

They know poverty from experience. They may have sold their
wedding ring for a drink and have hit bottom financially, physi-
cally, and spiritually. One former bank vice president ended up
on skid row, sleeping under bridges, and drinking cheap wine
out of a brown paper bag. He was sentenced by the court to

Cedar Hills Alcohol Treatment Center and, as he was preparing to leave at the end of his stay, he discussed with his counselor, one of our certificate graduates, his plans for the future. He said he wanted to go back into the banking business. His counselor said, "Yes, you start as a janitor in a bank." Now he is a vice president again.

I learn from alcoholics, too. Although not a member myself, I attend open meetings of Alcoholics Anonymous just because it is good for me to see lay people working harder at their spiritual life than I, who am supposed to be a professional.

One African-American woman came to my class one night to give the A.A. lecture, scared to death to be up in front of a largely white audience in a strange university. Her story was one of abject poverty, beatings, and squalor. By the time she finished it was clear that her beauty came from deep in her soul, which exuded a serenity that was unmistakably spiritual. The explanation came out when she revealed, quite simply and humbly, that she spends one solid hour every morning in prayer and meditation—the Eleventh Step of A.A. ☦

Chastity does not mean to be alone, but to share the riches of our solitude and loneliness and the prayer that such fragility draws out of us with the community and the people we serve. **Paul Janowiak, S.J.**

A Mystery
Paul Janowiak, S.J.

I believe in the fruitful, life-giving witness of chastity for the sake
of the Kingdom. I would like to see more young women and
young men consider the preciousness and excitement of such
a call today. That is a risky position to take considering the
confusion we have fostered over the centuries between religious
life and ordained ministry, seeing them, in terms of "chastity"
or "celibacy," as essentially the same. They are not the same,
and to consider them so is to muddle the value of each and
demean the whole richness of service in the Body of Christ.

It has been only in the last few years, when I began to unravel
that confusion for myself, that I have been able to imagine
concretely an ordained ministry that includes all women and
men—religious, married, and single. Only then did the realization of chastity as a powerful, healthy, and life-giving witness
of the Kingdom begin to deepen in me. And with this deepening
comes a genuine desire that the gift of a vowed life of chastity not
be lost or forgotten in the Church. We risk confusing its true
prophetic value by making celibacy a litmus test for presbyterial
ministry and by losing sight of the religious vow that is, in the
end, a surrender to love.

I must admit that I am perplexed by that deepening. Chastity
at many times is not easy. Often I have used this "coat" as
a shield to hide my fears and as a barrier to intimacy. Yet I believe
that God has used even this weakness as a path to a deeper
purification and conversion of my heart. And that conversion
is to love and to be loved in a way that is sacred and precious.

How can I say that? How dare I suggest that this vow is becoming a more sacred part of me? I can only say that I am very happy
in my life despite all its sorrows and failures and loneliness. I can
only say that I see men in this province whom I love and admire
and in whose presence God is alive and well, and I can attest that
chastity can be life-giving, fruitful, apostolic, and full of joy.

As I have begun to learn from the LaStorta community, with
whom I have been privileged to work and live for five years,
the more we share that intimacy of the heart with our brothers,

and risk sharing both the trials and the joys in a spirit of real brotherly affection, the more we begin to see that chastity is both a gift given to us and one that is shared in companionship with the community. Chastity does not mean to be alone, but to share the riches of our solitude and loneliness and the prayer that such fragility draws out of us with the community and the people we serve.

That leads to my final point. Solitude, loneliness, and the aching hunger for God are purified when you simply are drawn by those realities into the presence of God. It is God who embraces the boundaries of that sacred place deep within us and trusts us enough to ask us to surrender what seems so good and holy so that the world may glimpse another facet of the face of God.

It is a mystery. I am not very good at witnessing to its reality. Yet I hope that other young women and men will see the richness of this life that has no easy answers. When all men and women—single, celibate, and married—are welcomed into ordained ministry, I believe the real treasure and value of vowed chastity will be affirmed by more and more sisters and brothers risking to live by that call. ✝

*We were all standing in front of the
guest entrance to the monastery when
the clear thought and strong conviction
suddenly struck me that I should be,
and would be, a priest.*
Leo B. Kaufmann, S.J.

In Front of the Guest Entrance
Leo B. Kaufmann, S.J.

The origin of my vocation was so unlikely and idiosyncratic that I have always hesitated to talk about it. But Father Craig Boly's invitation, with the suggestion that this be written as a lenten penance, broke my resistance. I still do not rightly see how the grace given to me "can be passed on to others." But it could never have been meant for me alone.

When I was in the fourth grade my family had dinner at my aunt's in Mount Angel, Oregon. In the afternoon we visited their boy who was in the minor seminary at the Benedictine Abbey. We were all, both families, standing in front of the guest entrance to the monastery when the clear thought and strong conviction suddenly struck me that I should be, and would be, a priest. And it has never left me nor ever weakened. Until then I had not thought about the priesthood other than to ignore my mother's occasional hints and to resist the nuns' recruitment attempts.

After grade school I entered Mount Angel Seminary. All went well until my senior year when a monk returned from Solesmes intent on saving the world through Gregorian chant. The new abbot was of like mind. Since I am close to tone deaf I got kicked out of chant class with a grade of 59 percent.

As I licked my wounds I began to see nothing but trouble ahead if I stayed at Mount Angel with all its stress then on singing. But it bothered me that I could see the very spot where the Lord first called me. And if I went elsewhere what would become of that call?

I started reading about other religious orders. There were several books in the library that I remember about various religious orders: the Benedictines, the Dominicans, the Paulists, and the Jesuits. They all took a crack at the Jesuits. I wondered why. When I came to the one on the Jesuits by Archbishop Goodier, S.J., there was not a denigrating word about any other order but rather praise for all. I started reading everything

I could find, including Thomas Campbell's *The Jesuits 1534–1921: A History of the Society of Jesus from Its Foundation to the Present Time.*

I stayed at Mount Angel one more year for first-year college and made up my mind to apply for admission to the Society. My good friends, Bob Cieslinski, now pastor of Canby, Oregon, and the Charvet cousins, all of whom had Jesuit connections, did much to encourage me. And I must not forget to record an assist from Brother Johnny O'Brien, S.J., who visited Bob Cieslinski one Sunday and gave me all the facts, just the facts.

That I had received my call so clearly at Mount Angel still bothered me, but with the blessing of the seminary rector, I made the plunge. I regret to admit that I found it too embarrassing to tell him about my call's origin.

But my vocation survived the metamorphosis. It was a very tough adjustment from the moderate approach of the Benedictines to Father John Moffatt's higher flights. Father Moffatt was a popular Jesuit teacher. Yet I survived, and my vocation was never in question for me although it surely was for Father Moffatt and, I suspect, for many of my fellow novices who were, I thought, narrow-minded about the Church, unlike other Jesuits.

But I even got to like the novitiate, and I enjoyed every period of training progressively more—with the exception of first-year theology.

I do not know how straight a furrow I have plowed since that first moment sixty years ago when the Lord so firmly put my hand to the plow, but I do know that by his grace I never looked back. Maybe some day he will tell us why he chose me and maybe why he picked that moment and that place only to take me away later. ✝

*It has been a source of encouragement
that the Society of Jesus recognizes and
appreciates the vocation of monks and
of hermits (such as the Carthusians)
who spend their best energies "speaking
to the Lord about men and women
rather than speaking to men and
women about the Lord."*
Tony Lehmann, S.J.

The Society Would Not Expect a Man So Committed

Tony Lehmann, S.J.

Both the principle of the *magis* and the Jesuit motto ("Everything for the greater glory of God") are sources of daily strengthening, because they remind me of the firm conclusions I made earlier in my religious life. The sons of St. Bruno, who in the prologue to the Carthusian Statutes are exhorted to observe their way "more diligently in order to arrive more quickly at a greater love of God," would be the first to subscribe to the Society's goal of "greater glory to God."

It has been a source of encouragement that the Society of Jesus recognizes and appreciates the vocation of monks and of hermits (such as the Carthusians) who spend their best energies "speaking to the Lord about men and women rather than speaking to men and women about the Lord."

The Society would not expect a man so committed to leave such a vocation in order to become a Jesuit. On the other hand, Carthusians would be the last to suppose that a Carthusian could become a Jesuit.

Dom André Poisson, Father General of the Carthusians, told me once: "The Jesuits would never accept a Carthusian!" After I wrote to him of my experience of the *magis* as a continuum of the *diligentius, citius, perfectius* (more diligently, more quickly, more perfectly) principle of the Carthusian Statutes, he reconsidered.

Le plus of the Carthusian Statutes has become for me "the more" of the Constitutions as I read—quite "at home"—such exhortations from the General Examen as "more effectively; greater service of God; and to go farther in the Lord." I am continually amazed, by ways in which I never anticipated, that an ideal that seemed at one time to be so remote has proven to be so near. ✞

During my regency at Mpima Seminary in Zambia I was blessed to have as my spiritual director an elderly African monsignor whom we affectionately called Ambuye (the Chibemba word for "Lord"). **Chuck Schmitz, S.J.**

Walking with Ambuye
Chuck Schmitz, S.J.

I can honestly say that were it not for the timely challenges, cautions, and comforts of my spiritual directors, I probably would not be walking as a Jesuit today.

During my regency at Mpima Seminary in Zambia I was blessed to have as my spiritual director an elderly African monsignor whom we affectionately called *Ambuye* (the Chibemba word for "Lord"). Ambuye knew little of the classical treatises on prayer and the spiritual life; at least he never alluded to them. Instead, during our monthly get-togethers for spiritual direction, the monsignor would invite me to walk with him through the African bush. Along the way he would reference his comments by drawing my attention to a particular facet of nature.

On one occasion when I was feeling overworked, unappreciated, and spiritually stale (maladies common to all regents), Ambuye led me to a towering ant hill bristling with thousands of the tiny creatures. We quietly watched their frenzied comings and goings for what seemed like half an hour. The monsignor then turned to me and said, "To think they know nothing of Jesus." And we walked on.

Another time, shortly after I had returned from language school and was busting my buttons to impress everyone with my expertise in Chibemba, Ambuye took me to a chicken yard in a nearby village. Again we just silently observed. The rooster in this yard was a particularly obnoxious type: strutting, crowing, and pecking any hen that wandered too close. Suddenly a stick came flying out of one of the huts and thumped against the rooster's head. The monsignor smiled, his point was made, and we walked back to Mpima.

I vividly recall my last journey with Ambuye. It was several weeks before I was to return to the States for theology studies, and I was feeling anxious, somewhat depressed, and a little fearful. I was driving the monsignor to a remote village where he was to celebrate Sunday Mass. As we rounded a sudden corner on the dusty road, a pack of baboons lay directly ahead. I hit the brakes, and we came to a stop. The baboons took to the trees, hissing and screeching. When the dust settled, Ambuye tapped me on the shoulder and pointed to the trees. There I noticed that each of the younger baboons was wrapped protectively in the embrace of two or three adults. The monsignor winked and said, "There are arms waiting for you, too."

It has been nearly twenty years since my monthly walks with an elderly African monsignor who now walks with his Ambuye forever. Other spiritual directors have "walked" with me in the meantime, and for each of them I am extremely grateful. The frenetic ant, the cocky rooster, and the frightened baboon still show up in my life from time to time. Nevertheless, all of my spiritual directors have enabled me to continue my journey, walking as a companion of our Ambuye, Jesus. ✟

"Have you ever thought you might have a vocation?" he asked. Oh, oh! The secret was out. *James McGloin, S.J.*

A Jesuit Vocation Is About Love
James McGloin, S.J.

The possibility of a vocation had come into my head again. "But, I don't want to be a diocesan priest. That's for certain. I admire the Christian Brothers, who are my teachers. In fact, I might want to be a teacher myself—but do I want to join the Brothers? Maybe a few years of service in the Peace Corps would be just as good. Besides I enjoy going out. I like the dances. I like being with my family and friends. Yet why does this other idea keep popping into my head?"

Such were my thoughts as I finished high school at Butte Central. Did I talk with anyone about them? No, I just pushed them aside. "A year away from home at the university will help me think better," I said to myself, hoping that the vocation idea might go away.

At Gonzaga University in the early sixties all the Catholic students had to make a weekend retreat. A priest from the Spokane diocese (I've forgotten his name) was giving the particular retreat I attended. He spoke well, and I was moved. Again the questions of a vocation started to arise. During the retreat, I went to confession to the priest. He had absolved me, and I was about to leave. "Have you ever thought you might have a vocation?" he asked. Oh, oh! The secret was out. "I have sometimes," I replied. "Perhaps you should talk with someone about it," he said. "Maybe I should," I answered, as I left the box.

Back at Gonzaga University, wrapped in the studies, I forgot about the "maybe I should." Knock, knock. In came Father Jack Leary, the university president. "How are things going for you at the university, Jim? You're from Butte, aren't you? Great place. My father worked in the mines there before moving to Idaho. I see you at Mass fairly often. Did you ever think you might have a vocation?" Cornered again, I could not get off the hook so easily this time. Over the next few months, I talked with Father Leary again and also with two other fellow tribesmen from Butte: Fathers Jud Murray and Tim O'Leary. I finally decided to "try" the novitiate.

Father O'Leary, in a final interview, asked me why I wanted to enter. "I think I want to use my life so that I can be of service to people," I answered. "That's good, but more is needed," he said. "A Jesuit vocation is about love, a deep knowledge, and love of the Lord Jesus. Only then can you serve."

I have been learning that ever since.

I did not listen well to Jesus' direct invitation: "Come, follow me." However, he sent his friends to me, who said, "We have found the Messiah, come and see." I'm glad he sent them and they invited me. ✞

Throughout the years, the eyes of my heart continue to discern the deep bonds of humanity that link those who strive together, with God's help, for wholeness.
Bernie Tyrrell, S.J.

Bonds of Humanity
Bernie Tyrrell, S.J.

When I was asked to write about my "experience of solidarity
with the poor," I was initially discomfited. I thought, I have not
been to India or Africa or Central America. I have not worked
with the poor on skid row. How, then, can I honestly write about
my experience of solidarity with the poor?

But I realized that I have, in fact, met and ministered to and
been ministered to by many people who are economically poor
and "poor in spirit." I have also served and been served by many
individuals who are well off but truly "poor in spirit." It is in my
encounters over the past fourteen years with alcoholics and
others struggling with addictions that I have had my closest
contacts with the "poor."

When I was actively addicted to alcohol, I would on occasion
go into bars and drink with individuals who did not have my
educational or middle-class background. A few times I was
subjected to verbal abuse and even the threat of physical harm
by some who recognized that I was not "one of their own."
Because of my dress and manner of speech, I was viewed
as someone out "slumming." Unfortunately there was a certain
truth in this perception, because I did feel in the dim recesses
of my consciousness that I was somehow better than many of
those people I met.

My encounters over the years with individuals joined together
in a common struggle to come to grips with alcoholism and other
addictions have been quite another matter. I have met persons
of highly diverse racial, economic, and social backgrounds.
Many have been economically and culturally impoverished.
Some were economically poor before they became addicted to
alcohol. Others were rich in material goods at one time but had
lost "everything" as a result of their addiction. Still others were
materially well off but spiritually bankrupt. A common goal drew
us all together: the desire to achieve lasting sobriety.

Throughout the years, the eyes of my heart continue to discern
the deep bonds of humanity that link those who strive together,
with God's help, for wholeness. There is a common questing for

honesty, humility, and poverty of spirit. There is an ongoing struggle to get one's priorities straight. Most important, there is a real sense of friendship, of brotherly and sisterly concern for one another, regardless of racial, cultural, or social status.

In the crucible of my struggle with addiction I have been deeply blessed. I realize "in my gut" that I am no better than the beggar on the street asking for a handout. The beggar is my brother or my sister. I have come to know, respect, and care for people who are economically and culturally deprived. I have learned something of compassion, although I have a long way to go. I have met the *anawim* (Hebrew word meaning "the poor") of every strata of our society, and they continuously reveal to me the truth of the beatitude: "Blessed are the poor in spirit, for theirs is the kingdom of heaven" (Mt. 5:3). ☦

*When a brother asks sincerely, "How's it going?" I feel
I belong.* **Joe Small, S.J.**

Three Very Important Rooms
Joe Small, S.J.

It seems to me that in our Jesuit houses we have three very important rooms. These three rooms are important, because it is in them where we come together, where we gather, and where we are able to experience and live community in specific ways.

The first room is the chapel where we come together for prayer and for liturgy. I truly feel deeply supported and fortified when I sense my brothers want to be there. I sense a faith community when I hear expressed deep concerns about the community and the apostolic work. For me this is where I receive my deepest and strongest spiritual energy and support from my commitments.

The second place is the recreation room. Here we can come together and enjoy one another's company. For my sense of support in the rec room I need the feeling of being accepted and of being comfortable. I do feel a strong and deep refreshment doing my apostolic work when I experience an enjoyable session in the rec room.

The third place we come together is the refectory. We eat together. Better yet, we try to "dine" together. How supporting that can be if we take our time and truly enjoy one another's company.

I would like to add to the above reflections that certain words—what I will call "how you?" questions from community— are the source of strong support. When a brother asks sincerely, "How's it going?" I feel I belong, especially after coming back from some apostolic work and I hear, "Hey, Joe, welcome back, and how did it go?" Then I can say in my heart, "He really missed me, and he really cares about what is happening in my life." For me this is one of the strongest experiences of community support in my apostolic life.

In conclusion, one thing I have done in recent years during prayer for the members of my community is to list their names on a piece of paper. Then I go over each name and picture the person each morning and pray, "Jesus, in union with you, may we touch and heal _____" and then enter the name of the person. ✝

In the Jesuit community, it's the humanity, hospitality, and shared goals that aid me in my work and prayer.
Jim Swindal, S.J.

Through Its Absence More Than Its Presence
Jim Swindal, S.J.

I have probably discovered the impact and importance of the Jesuit community more through its absence than through its presence. I suppose I am, like many, afflicted with the habit of taking for granted the commonplace. Let me illustrate.

During my first year of regency at Bellarmine High School in Tacoma, Washington, a family of one of the students asked Jim Voiss, a classmate, and me to house-sit for them. We readily agreed. The duties were few and the privileges many. We had free rein over their well-stocked freezer, their color cable television, their Monte Carlo (with sunroof no less, though admittedly useless during the Tacoma winter), their pool table, and so on. A perfect hideaway from the very community from which I needed a break, right?

After two days I was ready to move back to Bellarmine. Despite having the serenity and privacy I thought I needed to forestall the February doldrums, I was restless. I found myself missing the tales of Jake Blase, a veteran Jesuit, about priests who said Mass wearing red jogging suits. I missed having to hunt for the *Time* magazine that was always mysteriously absent from the recreation room. I even missed the rattle of my radiator in the mornings. So you can imagine how happy I was to return after those three weeks away.

In the Jesuit community, it's the humanity, hospitality, and shared goals that aid me in my work and prayer. ✝

Rather than come to where I was, he asked me, without respite, to come to where he was. **Stephen Sundborg, S.J.**

A New Horizon of My Life
Stephen Sundborg, S.J.

I feel embarrassed by the question, What have been your experiences of solidarity with the poor?, because mine seem so paltry. And yet I know this solidarity is an essential dimension of our vocation as Jesuits. But I don't think I am alone in this feeling of embarrassment, this tension that the definition of what it means to be a Jesuit today creates in me and in us while our experience catches up with our hearts and convictions. Perhaps, therefore, it is salutary simply to admit this felt inadequacy without trying to justify it or to diminish the tension that I and, perhaps many of us, feel knowing what we are called to do but still not being quite ready yet in our choices and experiences.

For me the primary experience of solidarity with the poor was and is being with Jesus in prayer in the Spiritual Exercises. At the time of my tertianship long retreat, some ten years ago, I had a reorienting experience of Jesus. I had basically become accustomed in prayer and retreats to experience and therefore to look for the Jesus who would care for and nourish me. He would wash me, heal me, strengthen me, comfort and console me, and essentially come to wherever I was to minister to me. But in this retreat, try however hard I might, he just would not do this. From the first day to the last he insisted that he needed *my* care, *my* healing, *my* comfort, *my* washing, and *my* strengthening. Rather than come to where I was, he asked me, without respite, to come to where he was.

And what I came to realize was that he was in and with the poor asking for my care and that if I were to meet him I would need to go there. This realization formed the basis of my election, a reorientation of a fundamental attitude that did not entail specific actions but that opened up what would become a new horizon of my life. This may not seem to be much of an "experience of solidarity with the poor," but then again it may be so in a very radical way. It created a conviction of the heart that opened me to small ways of caring for Christ, where he is in the poor, beckoning. My inadequacy, my paltriness of experience, and my embarrassment derive from how, or more usually how I have not, acted upon what was given in grace.

The gift from that tertianship retreat seems to have been internal antennae to pick up how the Gospel is heard in a new way with the poor. What otherwise might have been a rather routine hearing of the Gospel I have found to be suddenly new and vital in the presence of the poor. I think, for example, of the Gospel heard, preached, and prayed on in the community Eucharistic celebrations in L'Arche houses. I come to these celebrations to proclaim and preach the Gospel but always find that these "handicapped" people and the assistants crack open the Gospels for me and allow me to hear them in a new way. They somehow take away defenses and the intellectualizing pretenses with their spontaneity and directness. The Good News seems more real and more direct.

When I was traveling around the province last year in preparation for the Procurators' Congregation, I began to be aware, quite keenly, where I could and where I could not really hear the Gospel. I think of places like Omak or St. Ignatius, Montana, where the Gospel felt surprisingly real. Perhaps even more so, after visiting Nativity House and that incredible block around St. Leo's in Tacoma, I was overwhelmed how powerful was the Gospel of the Sunday Eucharist. It is more than a feeling (yet also a feeling), more a conviction that Jesus is there and speaks more vitally there, at least to me. ✞

*There is a profoundly felt spirituality
that we have assimilated that makes
us companions.* **Dan Weber, S.J.**

Bonds That Transcended Separation
Dan Weber, S.J.

I entered the Jesuits for community and companionship. Having experienced interlocking friendships in my large family, in the U.S. Navy, and as a Gonzaga University boarder, I found companionship in the Society an answer to a longing and a very great joy in shared friendship.

Our large scholastic communities in formation years nurtured me in the hard days of study. But they were broken up by separations as we were sent to different missions and to new and smaller communities. The shared experiences, however, had created bonds that transcended separation. So today I feel especially close to Jack O'Leary in Africa, to Joe Retzel in St. Ignatius, Montana, to Tom Williams* in Lewiston, Idaho, and to Bill Dibb in Alaska. These are only a few names. For me, these men are never really apart, and when we get together we rebuild friendships in an instant. I can understand how Ignatius felt about Xavier far away in India.

My high school communities, where I have lived so long and in so many different places, are home for me now, but they, too, change regularly. Members come and go. Yet new, shared experiences create a bond. I also find this rooted companionship across the nation. When I go to a Jesuit Secondary Educational Association (J.S.E.A.) meeting, we Jesuits experience much joy in our shared experiences. We have instant community at national meetings. There is a profoundly felt spirituality that we have assimilated that makes us companions. It allows for differences of opinion and choice of work, but we are more united than divided. Thus, when I go to Seattle University or Gonzaga University, it is like a family homecoming. We are together in our apostolate no matter what our special service.

As I look back, I am happy I joined the Society of Jesus. I was asked to be a diocesan priest, but I knew I did not want to live alone. Community is my way to salvation. ✝

It has been during these years of living out of a suitcase that I have discovered the beauty of our Jesuit communities.
Chuck Suver, S.J.

Thank You Is Not Quite Enough
Chuck Suver, S.J.

For a long time I have searched for a way to express my gratitude to the houses of the province for their hospitality and support. My story is simple yet in many ways unique.

For the greater part of my senior year of high school, I lived in the old Jesuit faculty house at Seattle Preparatory. I was very much attracted to community life. There was so much harmony, enjoyment, and unity among the scholastics. I entered the Society after my senior year. I thoroughly enjoyed the large communities at the Mount in Spokane and at Alma in Los Gatos, California.

Shortly after tertianship, I reactivated, with the provincial's permission and support, the Jesuit mission band in our province. The first year I worked under a New York missioner, the second year under Father Curtis Sharp, Oregon province. Then for about three years I was on lend-lease to the Marine Corps. What I missed most during that interval was our Jesuit communities. As soon as I was discharged (honorably), I went to Alaska to give missions for Bishop Fitzgerald. For the next seven years I worked with Father Frank Toner, then for five years with Father Luke Kruezer. (Just in passing, I might add, the last fourteen years I've been on the road, too, working in marriage encounter and rediscovery).

Strangely enough, it has been during these years of living out of a suitcase that I have discovered the beauty of our Jesuit communities, from Port Townsend in Washington to Havre, Harlem, and Hays in Montana; from Seattle and Tacoma, Washington to Portland and Cave Junction, Oregon; from Spokane, Washington to Missoula, Montana; from Lewiston, Idaho to Pendleton, Oregon—sound like a travel agent? There's more: Ketchikan, Sitka, Juneau, Anchorage, Fairbanks, Nome, Holy Cross, Bethel in Alaska. In all of these places I have received the gracious and generous hospitality of the Society.

The whole point of this narrative is to express my sincere gratitude to those communities that have made me feel at home. Even when I was unable to alert them beforehand that I was coming, always I was received graciously, always I was made to feel that I belonged, always I was supported in the work I was doing. It just seems that "thank you" is so very little for so very much. ✝

To be in solidarity with the poor is, at its most personal level, the same as being in solidarity with my vows as a Jesuit and my desire as a Christian.
J. D. Whitney, S.J.

A Rich Young Man
J. D. Whitney, S.J.

If in polite society, one is cautioned against raising the subjects
of politics and religion, one is similarly cautioned in polite Jesuit
society to avoid the subject of solidarity with the poor.

Few topics seem as effective in bringing out the worst instincts
in many of us as this. When it is raised, our hypocrisy, our soph-
istry, our self-righteousness all rally to our defense as we attempt
to show either that (a) we are in the true ministry to the poor or
that (b) someone else is not. This, at least, is the reaction I find
in myself, and it leads me to wonder why I feel this way. What
is it about the call to solidarity with the poor that causes me and
many other Jesuits to squirm and rationalize our own ministries
or to stand in judgment over the "Jesuit" nature of another's
work? I think it has to do with the awareness of our own sinfulness that this call to solidarity requires.

To be in solidarity with the poor is, at its most personal level,
the same as being in solidarity with my vows as a Jesuit and my
desire as a Christian. The vow of poverty does not begin with
the Thirty-second General Congregation, and when I am aware
how far I am from the true living of this vow, I am aware how far
I am from the loving Christ who calls me to this life. Of course,
I can, and do, justify myself by saying that all I own belongs to
the Society. But does "common ownership" get any of us off
the hook for living as well as we do? Perhaps if I had vowed
"common life" instead of "poverty" this would bother me less.
Unfortunately, however, I did vow poverty, and my distance from
it makes me uncomfortable with the topic of solidarity with the
poor for, in my heart, I know that my distance from the poor
is the same as my distance from Christ.

So, I feel uncomfortable. So what? Should I give up my office
and my job in this upper-middle-class university and go to work
on the reservation or on the streets of Seattle? Maybe. The time
I spent on the streets of Tacoma or in the Jesuit Volunteer Corps
(JVC) in Alaska certainly brought me a humble awareness of
Christ's presence among the poor and the need and the right

they have for the promise of the Gospel. So, perhaps, this is the way to get rid of my discomfort.

On the other hand, since God has given me a great gift in my education, do I not have an obligation to teach young men and women that society can have a human face or to counsel them at times when Christ is as absent from them as he is from the poor? I cannot help but think I do. There is real value here, real purpose in this ministry. But what of solidarity with the poor?

Perhaps I could get rid of my discomfort by seeing what I do as, in some way, an act of solidarity with the poor. After all, these people who do not know God are "spiritually" poor, aren't they? And if they become the leaders of society, what they learn from me will affect the poor, will it not? There is a truth in these arguments, but there is also something that smacks of rationalization, just as there is also something that smacks of oversimplification in the idea of quitting to work with the "real" poor. Neither alternative offers a clear solution to the discomfort that the call to solidarity with the poor raises.

Maybe the truth is that a call to solidarity with the poor is meant to make me uncomfortable—not to make me hypocritical, not to make me self-righteous—but to make me uncomfortable. Like the rich young man to whom Christ spoke in the Scriptures, perhaps I am meant to be troubled because I am very wealthy, but unlike him, I need not go away sad. On the contrary, I need to stay with Jesus and embrace my discomfort as a sign of his gentle pulling me toward himself.

There have been and will be times when I turn my discomfort into anger or into cynicism, but without it I would be incapable of realizing my own incompleteness, my own sinfulness. I need to get closer to the poor in my work and in my heart. I need constantly to return on vacations or in my spare time to work among the powerless not because it relieves my discomfort, but because it heightens it. For me this pain, this discomfort, is the "happy fault," the *felix culpa*, that draws me from what I am to what, with the Lord's help, I have yet to be. ✝

*I've dealt with life, as with waffle batter,
by molding it into intelligible experience.*
Rick Ganz, S.J.

Only in This Experience of Being Stripped of All Strength

Rick Ganz, S.J.

I like waffles for breakfast. At least twice a week I'll stoke the waffle iron, blend some batter, and, within moments, rejoice in the possession of a crisp square waffle; a square neatly divided by the iron into four smaller squares. I understand waffles. I grasp the process of making them. I know that so much batter will yield so much waffle. I recognize a good result from a bad result.

The waffle-event says something about me and the way I've dealt with living through the years. In living, I've striven for a good result. I've tried to measure the significance of things. As I've mastered a recipe, I have applied myself to grasping the nature of things by perceiving their structures. I've dealt with life, as with waffle batter, by molding it into intelligible experience. Down the years I've found a certain stability, a predictability in living, a security.

Yet I hate this kind of living. In fact, I'm bone-weary of it. I hope that I've had quite enough of it. In recent years I've recognized how far the waffle-event is from reality, and how much I desire to accept life as it is: unpredictable, full of motion and emotion, insecure, untamable, huge, vivid, solid, wild, exhilarating, full of wonder. In short: alive! To that degree, I've put aside wrestling with reality—dealing with it, molding it, pressing it, and controlling it. Thus, I have understood better the Spiritual Exercises and, in particular, the "rules" for discernment presented therein.

How? The rules made little sense to me living at a distance from reality. What meaning could discernment have to me who lacked the freedom to receive life as it came? Who dealt with life by limiting it, by molding it, by controlling its influence on my carefully established security? "None," I say. The question about discernment was first asked when I had been, by grace, led out of my self-established security into the wild turbulence of reality, where I had no other surety but faith in the Faithful One. Only in

this experience of being stripped of all strength, of having all my
security swept away, of having nothing left but trust in God,
only then could I ask, How can I know my way in all this? It was
precisely in this context that the rules for discernment began to
mean something to me.

The Spiritual Exercises have meant more and more to me,
especially in recent years. In them I have seen a way of freedom:
a way of living in faith without controlling and dealing with life.
As a result of having found this treasure, I have been able
to share its extraordinary richness with others, especially in
spiritual direction. ♱

The street people who walk by my window each morning at 6:00 A.M., leaving the night shelter to head to the soup kitchen for breakfast, tell me of the lack of priority in our society for meeting the basic needs of the poor.
Peter Henriot, S.J.

A Chance to Meet Jesus
Peter Henriot, S.J.

During the long weeks of the Thirty-third General Congregation,
I felt many moments of deep consolation, particularly as I saw
the direction of our faith and justice mission strongly confirmed
through the lived experiences and prayerful discernment of
Jesuits from around the world who were represented there.
But I must be honest and acknowledge that I also felt moments
of significant desolation. These occurred most often when we
discussed our vow of poverty and our option for the poor.
At these times, the air was heavy with confusion, discouragement, and defensiveness. It seems clear that for all of us
"solidarity with the poor" is an immense challenge.

For me, the challenge takes names and faces. In the Washington, D.C., inner-city neighborhood where I live, Ed Cross's daily
visits to our community remind me of the loneliness of the
elderly poor. Mrs. Wills' working hard to hold down two jobs
with minimum pay in order to raise many children and grandchildren shows me the strength of poor women. Diablo, thirteen
years old and struggling with reading lessons in the local school,
teaches me about problems of the poor with education. The
street people who walk by my window each morning at 6:00 A.M.,
leaving the night shelter to head to the soup kitchen for breakfast, tell me of the lack of priority in our society for meeting the
basic needs of the poor.

Why would I want to be in solidarity with these people?

A graced experience I had several years ago returns to haunt
me with an answer to that question.

I made my tertianship in Latin America in the mid-seventies.
Studying Spanish in Bolivia for a few months, I appreciated the
fact that an easy way to learn a new language is to practice it with
small children. They are very eager to help, correct, and make fun
of adults! One day I accompanied an older Jesuit to a residence
where very poor orphans lived. As I walked through the crowd
of youngsters who ran up to talk to me, one little boy in particular was trying to get my attention. He was clearly very poor,
shabbily dressed, and he had a bad limp. I soon realized that

he also was retarded. Because he was not going to be of much help for my practice of Spanish, I moved away from him to seek out some other youngsters.

Slowly, the young boy turned and sought out the older Jesuit who was with me. The Jesuit picked him up and asked him, "*¿Cómo te llamas, niño?* (What's your name, little boy?") I remember to this day when the little boy answered. "*¡Me llamo Jesús!* (My name is Jesus!")

I missed a chance to meet Jesus, because I turned aside from an opportunity of solidarity with the poor. ✝

I believe Ignatius understood how the fruit of prayer ripens best when exposed to the senses—when soaked in our gut-wrenching, heart-swelling emotions.
Brad Reynolds, S.J.

I Am Most Moved by What I Can See, Hear, Touch, Taste, and Smell
Brad Reynolds, S.J.

Conversion is gut-wrenching and heart-swelling. Jacob pops his hip, Jonah flails inside his whale, Paul topples from his horse. St. Thomas of Aquinas' articles and Bernard Lonergan's insights might explain the force behind the effect, but they don't flood the tear ducts or flare the nostrils, not like Picasso's *Guernica* or Barber's *Adagio*.

In my prayer and in my work, Ignatius' Application of the Senses makes the best sense. I am most moved by what I can see, hear, touch, taste, and smell. I do not understand how cornea, eardrum, epidermis, tongue, and nostrils change the heart, but they do. What is important for my prayer is that they do.

Photographs and paragraphs seem to work best when they too flop the heart over on its side. Likewise, I don't know how they do it and will leave the explanations to someone else.

I believe Ignatius understood how the fruit of prayer ripens best when exposed to the senses—when soaked in our gut-wrenching, heart-swelling emotions.

If, in prayer, the senses bring the soul alive, then can't they draw the soul into prayer itself? Not knees-on-the-ground, hands-clasped, lips-whispering devotions but a powerful lurching out of self and into something, someone else. Isn't that bringing the Word alive, proclaiming it in technicolor visions, symphonies, taste-treats, flying tackles, and the scent of fresh baked bread?

This is the stuff that saturates a soul. When we can wrench guts and swell hearts, I do believe we are closer to the Divine. ✢

I choose to remain, however, because I firmly believe that God speaks to poets as loudly as to prophets, and that if only everyone would read Homer correctly everything would be okay. **Kevin Connell, S.J.**

To Poets as Well as to Prophets
Kevin Connell, S.J.

I think I joined the Society of Jesus, because I was born too late
for the Trojan War.

I approached with considerable trepidation Peter Ely's* secretary in April of 1981 because, having spent four years around the
Jesuits of "the other" Bellarmine in San Jose and two more years
at Gonzaga, I firmly believed that the Jesuits were engaged upon
the noblest, harshest, and most exciting quest I could imagine:
Saving the world by saving the minds of themselves and those
around them from sloth and ignorance.

These incredibly talented people like Warren Wright, Fred
Schlatter, Jon Fuller, David Leigh*, and others who had sacrificed
the worldly success they could easily have enjoyed struck me as
something like the Knights Templar with typewriters. Although
I did not always agree with their beliefs, I was consistently
impressed by their willingness to devote themselves to them
entirely in what I saw then as the utterly-unlivable-by-mortal-
beings life of the vows.

I first discussed my attraction to the Society during my senior
year at Bellarmine. My best friend and I were discussing our
future plans, and I admitted to having considered the Jesuits.
He encouraged me to talk to the scholastics or the "somethings."
I don't think I even knew that word then.

Of course, I didn't in part because I hoped the desire would
go away and in part because I didn't feel worthy of "the call."

Despite my best attempts in Spokane at a romantic agnosti-
cism that would have given Captain Ahab second thoughts, this
attraction toward the Society persisted throughout my two years
at "Godzilla U" (as Peter Ely taught me to call it when I swam into
him head-on at the pool one day). I spent my share of tearful
vigils in the Jesuit House chapel and told my parents I'd decided
to apply a year before I actually did. (Smart people that they are,
they never mentioned it again until I did.)

Finally at the end of my sophomore year and nine more
months of frantic academic and dramatic activity (more tearful
vigils) that left my 5'10" Malvolio weighing 135 lbs. in costume,

I finally admitted to myself that I was looking for something more out of life than school or the careers in education or theater that I was considering offered me. I still felt somehow beneath, far beneath, the call I exhibited toward the Society. However, when I learned that a friend of mine had applied to the California province I figured, "What the hell? I'll apply. They'll turn me down. I'll get royally self-righteous, and this whole thing will be out of my system."

Much to my surprise I was accepted and, still feeling dubious about my motives, I came to the novitiate.

Since then my rather bizarre call has continued. I remain uncomfortable with specifically religious language, I consider the current papal regime bigoted and paranoid, and I haven't stayed awake for an entire liturgy in years. I choose to remain, however, because I firmly believe that God speaks to poets as loudly as to prophets, and that if only everyone would read Homer correctly everything would be okay. Further, I know that unless I do something about this as a Jesuit I will have failed to "follow my bliss," as the late mythologist Joseph Campbell put it. Doubts continue to this very day. A voice in my head whispers, "You're not trying to save the world, you're running from it"; "You're about as religious as Herod the Great on a bad day, what would the Son of God want with you?"

Fortunately, confirmations crop up as well. Pat O'Leary* and GU's Bob Egan occasionally convince me that God does not enjoy making people feel rotten about themselves. Scholastics and students at St. Michael's told me that my "secular humanism" made me a more attractive Jesuit. Students and faculty at Jesuit High liked me even when I screwed up the basketball scoreboard or missed an entrance while filling in for Fezziwig in *A Christmas Carol.*

My eyes are a lot less dazzled than they were in 1981, and God knows we are more than a few ships short of a thousand, but every once in awhile the topless towers of Ilion (Troy) still shine through the mist. ✝

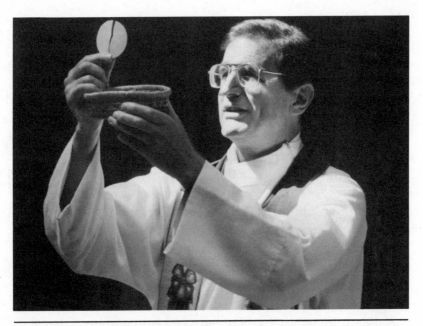

I started to understand that this is where I was meant to be, somewhere between God and my friends.
Pat Twohy, S.J.

A Hidden Journey
Pat Twohy, S.J.

I once read that when the actress Bette Davis saw her first real
play, she said to herself, "That is what I am!"

When I was twelve I was asked to help a priest do a funeral
Mass for another young boy, who had slipped and fallen on the
ice under the back wheels of a school bus. His head was crushed.
All of my friends from both the Catholic and public schools came
to the funeral. Suddenly I found myself standing there in my
cassock and surplice, holding the thurible. I had never stood so
close to death. I can still see the brown casket in front of me and
sense the presence of the priest praying on my left, the incense
rising in front of us. I had never stood in such a way before God
and before my friends, who were crying.

Feeling ran like lightning up through my chest and throat.
One minute I would start to cry; then I was afraid I would laugh.
I couldn't understand what I was feeling, but I was starting to
KNOW something. I started to understand that this is where
I was meant to be, somewhere between God and my friends;
not completely with God and not completely with my friends.
I felt caught somewhere in between, now going up towards God,
now reaching out to my friends, belonging to both, but belonging in a most intense manner to myself, to my vision, and to my
ability to dream. I belonged partly to this world and partly to the
world of spirits, always squinting at this world but trying to see
what was just beyond it.

In this way I began to know I was gifted and special beyond
the reach of anyone's praise, or criticism, or expectations of
me. I simply knew I had a hidden journey to make, a journey
as insubstantial and inexplicable as the incense smoke that
appeared for a moment in the soft December light and then
disappeared into the darkness above the wooden beams of the
church loft.

This was not a story I ever told anyone about nor a vision that
I ever tried to explain to someone who might understand. It was
simply a journey I began as a young man and have continued to
this day, no matter how confusing or how dark the path, no

matter how difficult the climb up, beyond all friendships with the living and the dead.

This has been the journey of a fragile, gentle person, a hidden person, who knew only how to dream and how to be alone. It has been a journey nourished by the example of my grandmothers—Methodist and Catholic—and my parents, sisters, relatives, and friends, who have loved me without reserve. It has been a journey guided by the witness of diocesan priests and Father Francis Rouleau, a Jesuit missionary in China, who appeared with all the power and mystery of an Elijah at the death of my Catholic grandmother and by the lives of all my Jesuit teachers and companions over the years.

There never were adequate or compelling "reasons" for me to be a priest. It has always been something different than that. It is more like a growing awareness, a kinship with a yearned for Presence beyond all my powers of knowing. Yet I have felt this Presence since I was young, and it still seems most natural to want to be drawn into this Mystery. It is a joy to know that there are companions for such a journey. And it still seems right and good to want to talk with other human beings about the frightening darkness and the warm, compelling Light that we all discover in the center of our being, in the depths of our hearts and minds, and in the midst of our journey. ✟

Contributors

J. K. Adams has taught at Jesuit High School in Portland, Oregon, conducting classes in Christian morality and Ignatian spirituality to juniors. He now studies theology at the Jesuit School of Theology at Berkeley.

Craig Boly is dean of St. Michael's Institute in Spokane. He is associate professor of Religious Studies at Gonzaga University and edited the six volumes of *Laborers in the Harvest.*

Phil Boroughs served as the assistant to the novice director before earning a Ph.D. in spirituality from the Jesuit School of Theology at Berkeley and has taught theology at Gonzaga University. At present, he is a writer in Seattle.

Peter Byrne worked as pastor of St. Leo's in Tacoma, at the downtown chapel in Portland, and at St. Joseph's in Seattle. He is rector of St. Michael's Institute for Jesuit scholastics, studying philosophy and theology.

L. Patrick Carroll has served the past seven years as pastor of St. Leo's parish in Tacoma, Washington. He worked as copastor at St. Joseph's parish, Seattle, and as rector and president of Bellarmine Preparatory in Tacoma. He has authored five books of spirituality.

Dick Case serves as president of Gonzaga Preparatory School in Spokane, Washington.

Frank Case is the regional assistant to the Father General for the United States. He has been provincial, rector at Seattle University, and a member of the faculty of the Albers School of Business at Seattle University, where he taught courses in economics and business ethics.

Jerry Chapdelaine is the rector at Bellarmine Preparatory in Tacoma. He conducted retreats at Loyola Retreat House in Portland from 1968 to 1980. From 1980 to 1986, he administered at Gonzaga Preparatory in Spokane. The largest part of his ministry has been with adolescents.

Jerry Cobb teaches English at Seattle University.

Tom Colgan works as coexecutive director of Kateri Northwest Ministry Institute, a ministry training institute for Native Americans. Tom is a counselor and a Chemical Dependency Specialist II, who enjoys watercolor and doing spiritual direction.

Kevin Connell studies at the Weston School of Theology in Cambridge, Massachusetts. He has taught high school English and drama, performed for four seasons at the Idaho Shakespeare Festival, worked with homeless teenagers, and currently does volunteer work with the AIDS Action Committee of Boston.

Tom Connolly has worked since his ordination in 1963 with Native Americans in Colville and Spokane, Washington, and in Coeur d'Alene, Idaho.

Pat Conroy is assigned to Georgetown University in the Office of Campus Ministry and is developing an interfaith retreat program for freshmen at the university. For five years before coming to Georgetown, he was the pastor of four parishes on the Colville and Spokane Indian reservations in Washington State.

Michael L. Cook is associate professor of Religious Studies at Gonzaga University. He taught Christology at the Jesuit School of Theology at Berkeley and was rector of St. Michael's Institute.

Frank Costello is vice president at Gonzaga University with a special mission to the law school. He was the academic vice president at both Seattle University and Gonzaga University and rector of the Jesuit community at Gonzaga University.

Gene Delmore acts as the visiting priest for four villages centered around St. Mary's on the lower Yukon in Alaska and is affiliated with the Native Ministry Training Program that started this year at St. Mary's. He has done retreat work in Anchorage, parish work in Fairbanks, and campus ministry at Seattle University.

Andy Dufner has done research, writing, and teaching in theoretical physics, theology, and science for most of his Jesuit life. He is now engaged in spiritual direction and pastoral physics at the Nestucca Sanctuary on the Oregon coast.

George Dumais has taught high school and administered residences for the past sixteen years for developmentally disabled women and men in Missoula, Montana.

Arthur L. Dussault was vice president emeritus at Gonzaga University until his death on March 17, 1991. He was vice president for thirty-two years. He was officially Gonzaga's public relations ambassador and spent his sixty-two years at Gonzaga planning and executing campus expansion and beautification. He was a DeSmet Medal awardee and charter member of the university's Athletic Hall of Fame.

Peter B. Ely is pastor of St. Joseph parish in Seattle, Washington. He was academic vice president of Gonzaga University in Spokane, Washington, for twelve years. He has taught theology at Gonzaga and was chair of Gonzaga's Department of Religious Studies.

John Endres teaches Old Testament studies at the Jesuit School of Theology in Berkeley. He has authored a book on biblical spirituality, has taught high school, and has ministered in a parish setting.

Paul Fitterer is the assistant provincial for formation and coordinator for secondary education in the Oregon province. He has taught and counselled in high schools and universities in both Spokane and Seattle.

Patrick M. Flannigan ministers to senior citizens at St. Rita's in Tacoma, Washington. He was an administrator for the previous twenty years at Jesuit High School in Portland, Oregon.

Rick Ganz is a doctoral student at the Institutum Patristicum Augustinianum in Rome, where he continues a study of Dionysius the Areopagite (sixth century Syria). He has taught in both high school and university and was for three years the assistant novice director in the Oregon province.

Ed Goldian is pastor of St. Francis Xavier parish in Missoula, Montana. Before becoming pastor he was a chaplain in a mental hospital, in a medical facility, and in a prison. He taught high school for seventeen years.

William Hayes has been president of Jesuit High School in Portland, Oregon, for the past seven years. He has taught high school and has spent twenty-eight years in educational administration.

Peter Henriot founded the Center for Concern in Washington, D.C. He is the director of the Jesuit Theological Reflection Center in Lusaka, Zambia.

John Hurley is executive vice president of Gonzaga Preparatory School in Spokane, Washington. A graduate of the class of 1932, Hurley returned to his alma mater as assistant principal in 1947. In 1953, he assumed fund-raising duties for the high school's new campus. His fund-raising efforts resulted in a new campus, a new Jesuit residence, and a $3 million plus financial aid endowment.

J. Patrick Hurley is administrator of St. Philomena's in Des Moines, Washington. He has been pastor in Seattle, Tacoma, and Yakima, and also served as provincial assistant for Social and Parish Ministries in the Oregon province.

Paul Janowiak was on the pastoral staff of St. Ignatius parish in Portland, Oregon, for the past five years and was a member of the La Storta apostolic Jesuit community there. He is currently doing graduate studies in liturgy and homiletics at the Graduate Theological Union in Berkeley, California.

Leo B. Kaufmann is an associate pastor in Milwaukee, Oregon. He has taught high school and college, been a seminary professor, province prefect of studies, province consultor, and rector at Seattle University.

Tony Lehmann lived as a Carthusian hermit for twelve years before joining the Jesuits in 1972. He acted as chaplain for the Gonzaga-in-Florence program before assuming the chaplaincy of the alumni association at Gonzaga University.

David Leigh teaches English and directs the honors program and the core curriculum at Seattle University. He has taught high school at Gonzaga Preparatory and eleven years of English at Gonzaga University, where he also served as rector of St. Michael's Institute from 1976 to 1982.

Bill LeRoux has been at Seattle University for thirty-two years. During that time, he taught theology and was dean of the College of Arts and Sciences. For the past nine years, he has been raising money for Seattle University.

James McGloin is provincial of the Jesuit province of Zambia. He has taught in secondary school and in teachers' training college in Zambia prior to his present appointment.

Mark McGregor teaches Latin American history and social studies at Seattle Preparatory in Seattle, Washington. He has coordinated school trips to Washington, D.C., and South America and coached girls' soccer. He enjoys being a Jesuit Volunteer Corps support person.

Michael McHugh, after years of teaching and parish work in Portland and Seattle, is now happily at home among the Blackfeet Indians in Browning, Montana.

Roy Mann is a regent in Spokane, Washington, at the Kateri Northwest Ministry Institute, where he works as fund-raiser and teaches a dance-movement and prayer class. Interested in the performing arts, Roy has directed a short play for a Honduran theater troupe and has choreographed sacred dances in church settings. He currently is a member of the Conservatory Ballet Theater in Spokane.

James N. Meehan is administrator of St. Olaf Church in Poulsbo, Washington. He directed the Search Retreat program at Gonzaga University. After finishing a doctorate in sociology at Stanford, he taught college, became provincial assistant for formation, and served as president of Jesuit High School in Portland, Oregon.

Fred Mercy is a Jesuit brother who ministers as pastoral associate at St. Joseph Church, Yakima, Washington.

Gordon Moreland is director of the House of Prayer for Priests in Orange, California. As a former Oregon province novice director, he is well known as a retreat master and spiritual director. In recent years, he has worked primarily with priests and bishops.

Jack Morris founded the Jesuit Volunteer Corps. He is pastoral administrator for Our Lady of Mount Virgin parish in Seattle and staffs the Jesuit Shalom Center.

Jake Morton is the pastor responsible for parishes on the Spokane reservation at Wellpinit, Ford, and West End. Since his ordination in 1975, he has worked with Native Americans.

John V. Murphy has been a high school principal, rector, province level administrator, and marriage and family counselor. He is superior of the senior Jesuit community at Seattle University.

John Navone is professor of biblical theology at the Gregorian University in Rome and at Seattle University summer school. His fifteenth book, *Seeking God in Story* (Liturgical Press, 1990), is his most recent contribution to narrative theology.

Patrick B. O'Leary formed Jesuits for the Society as novice director, then as rector of St. Michael's Institute. After two years at St. Joseph's parish in Seattle, he became rector of the Jesuit House community at Gonzaga University.

Brad Reynolds is vocation director for the Oregon province. He is also a freelance journalist with work published in such publications as *National Geographic.*

David Rothrock met Mother Teresa and Jean Vanier while studying theology in France. Since then he has been chaplain with the L'Arche movement in the United States, Europe, Canada, and India.

James E. Royce is professor emeritus of psychology and founding professor of addiction studies at Seattle University. He has authored books on philosophical psychology, alcoholism, and professional ethics, and has received national honors in both the psychology and alcoholism fields.

Chuck Schmitz worked as an educator and missionary in Zambia before returning to the United States. He is the rector of the Jesuit community at Gonzaga Preparatory School in Spokane.

Joe Small taught high school for twenty-five years, was rector of Jesuit High School in Portland for seven years, and is now in his fifth year of directing retreats and doing spiritual direction at Loyola Retreat House in Portland, Oregon.

Stephen Sundborg, formerly assistant professor of theology and rector of the Jesuit community at Seattle University, is now the provincial superior of the Oregon Province of the Society of Jesus. He holds a doctorate in spirituality from the Gregorian University in Rome and worked especially in areas of Ignatian spirituality, religious experience East and West, and mysticism.

Chuck Suver lives in the Jesuit community at Bellarmine Preparatory School in Tacoma, Washington. He worked for fourteen years with the mission band, was Navy chaplain for the Marine Corps for three years, and was pastor of St. Aloysius parish in Spokane for six years.

Jim Swindal is pursuing a doctorate in philosophy at Boston College. He has taught high school, done parish work, and has worked with evangelization and youth groups.

Pat Twohy lives with the Swinomish tribe on Puget Sound. He is a chaplain to all native peoples in the archdiocese of Seattle. He has lived and worked with Pacific Northwest tribes for the past seventeen years and has authored the book, *Finding a Way Home: Indian and Catholic Spiritual Paths of the Plateau Tribes.*

Bernie Tyrrell is professor of philosophy and religious studies at Gonzaga University and is a member of the pontifical faculty at St. Michael's Institute. He is widely known for his books on Christotherapy.

J. Kevin Waters is dean of the College of Arts and Sciences at Gonzaga University. He was a professor of fine arts at Seattle University from 1981 to 1983. He also served as acting academic vice president at Gonzaga University from 1985 to 1986. His musical compositions in recent years include two operas and a dozen works for theater.

Dan Weber is president of Bellarmine Preparatory School in Tacoma, Washington. This is the fifteenth year of his term, preceded by six years as president of Gonzaga Preparatory in Spokane and a teaching career in Jesuit high school religion programs.

J. D. Whitney, presently studying for his M.Div. at Jesuit School of Theology at Berkeley, has taught philosophy for the last three years at Seattle University. Although raised in California, John joined the Oregon province after spending time teaching English at St. Mary's High School, Alaska, while in the Jesuit Volunteer Corps.

Thomas G. Williams has taught in high school, been a high school administrator in Seattle and Tacoma, and has worked in parishes in the Northwest. Recently he was pastor of Sacred Heart Church in Christiana, Jamaica. He is now superior of the Regis community, Spokane.

Glossary

Carthusians: The Carthusian Order is a purely contemplative monastic order that was founded in 1084 by St. Bruno. The name Carthusian is derived from the Latin word *cartusia*, which means chartreuse, and comes from the Chartreuse mountains in the French Alps, where the first hermits lived their solitary and austere lives.

Carthusian Statutes: St. Bruno did not intend to found a new monastic order; thus the inspiration for the succeeding generations of Carthusians was the example of his life, which was entirely "hidden in the Face of God." Eventually the customs of the hermits were compiled in 1127. This primitive legislation was supplemented by ordinances of the general chapters. On several occasions, the ordinances were gathered together in a single edition of statutes.

Catholic Worker: In 1933 Dorothy Day founded in New York City a monthly newspaper called the *Catholic Worker.* Its intention was to make known the social teachings of the Church. The paper called for the practice of the works of mercy and the establishment of houses of hospitality. During the economic breakdown of the 1930s, dedicated Catholic workers established scores of houses of hospitality across the country.

Celibacy: The renunciation of marriage undertaken for some greater value such as a complete dedication of one's life to God or of service to neighbor. Roman Catholic priests embrace a life of celibacy as a condition for greater freedom in the service of God.

Chastity: The moral virtue that moderates and regulates the sexual appetite in humans. Jesuits and other religious living in community make a vow of chastity. The vow promises not only that the Jesuit will not marry, but that all his energy for love will be dedicated to honoring God and serving the people of God.

Christology: The study of Jesus the Christ from the point of view of faith, seeking, and understanding. The focus is on discovering how the historical Jesus of Nazareth became identified as the risen Christ of faith and how this identity came to be known by Jewish converts and eventually the entire gentile world.

Christotherapy: The healing process discovered and articulated by Bernie Tyrrell, S.J., in his books *Christotherapy I* and *Christotherapy II*. The healing process is based on a discernment called "mind fasting and spirit feasting."

Company: The Society of Jesus, or Jesuits, is also known as the Company of Jesus, taken from the Spanish *compañíos*, which means "those who share bread with one another."

Contemplation for Learning to Love Like God: The key exercise in the fourth and final week of the Spiritual Exercises of St. Ignatius Loyola. Joseph Tetlow, S.J., in his book, *Choosing Christ in the World, A Handbook*, explains: "First, love is act, not talk; it shows itself in the deed done, not simply in words spoken. Second, love works itself out in mutual sharing, so that the lover always gives to and receives from the beloved—everything: gifts, money, conviction, honors, positions."

Dorothy Day: Day was a freelance writer from Chicago who founded the *Catholic Worker* newspaper in New York City in 1933. She helped start houses of hospitality for unemployed and homeless women and men. Prior to the outbreak of World War II, she advocated pacifism and a policy of unilateral disarmament and nonresistance. She became the voice of Catholic conscientious objectors both during the war and afterward. Day moved thousands of people to a better life by her books and articles, particularly by her saintly example of love for the least of Christ's sisters and brothers.

Discernment: Jesus gives the lead in recognizing the desires within us. Discernment involves the motives that move us and the desires that draw us to act. Spiritual discernment sifts through these motives and desires in order to discover which movements originate in God and which movements derive from human passion.

Enneagram: An ancient oral and written tradition derived from the Middle East and the Sufi movement of the Islamic faith that describes nine personality types and their interrelationships. The Enneagram is a system for understanding personality types that is based on normal and healthy behavior rather than on pathology alone.

Examen: The Examen or the Examination of Conscience in the Spiritual Exercises is a brief prayer recited in the middle and at the end of the day in order to "check" a person's behavior. If a person wants to make a habit of something, then the individual would focus upon that particular action for the examen. This is a way of reviewing what the person has done during the day.

First Principle and Foundation: The initial consideration of the Spiritual Exercises of St. Ignatius. The First Principle and Foundation states that each human being is so put together that by praising, honoring, and living according to the will of God, he or she will safely reach the kingdom of God, the original purpose of human life.

First Week: The Spiritual Exercises are divided into four weeks, or units of time, for prayer. Since each of the four weeks has its own specific grace attached to it, sometimes it takes more time or less time to receive the grace of the week. The grace of the first week is to see sin in all its ugliness and to see the mercy of God inviting us to turn away from sin.

General Congregation: The governing legislative body of the Society of Jesus, automatically convened upon the death of the General Superior, who is designated superior for life. The General Superior can call a general congregation to enact legislation for the good order of the Society or in response to the Church's initiatives through such events as the Second Vatican Council or the recent reform of the Church's Code of Canon Law. Since the founding of the Society of Jesus, there have been only thirty-three general congregations, the most recent in 1981.

Horizons for Justice: A program for Jesuits in North America during the 1970s in which Jesuits visited Central and South American countries for eight weeks during the summer. Organized by Harold Bradley, S.J., of Georgetown University, the privately-funded program enabled up to thirty Jesuits per summer to visit such countries as Guatemala, Nicaragua, and El Salvador. It provided an opportunity for Jesuits to be with poor people and to experience life on their terms in order to bring back to their communities in North America a heightened consciousness of the reality of poverty.

Junior Encounter program: A retreat program for juniors in high school. High school seniors plan the talks and organize the practical planning for meals, lodging, and clean up. With the guidance of the school staff, the seniors help the juniors open up about themselves, their problems, and their life of prayer.

Juniorate: The phase of Jesuit training that used to come immediately after the novitiate (see **novitiate**). Once the young man had pronounced perpetual vows, he began his Jesuit life by dedicating himself to the study of humanities. The juniorate comprised courses in classical languages, history, literature, drama, and mathematics with special emphasis placed on developing written and spoken skills. The juniorate originally lasted two years (it now is called the collegiate program and lasts approximately three years), and credits earned during this phase could be used toward the undergraduate college degree for men who had entered the Society out of high school.

L'Arche movement: After finishing a doctorate in philosophy in Paris in the early 1960s, the Canadian Jean Vanier decided to dedicate his life to caring for emotionally and mentally handicapped men. As he invited others to share his love for the disabled, the L'Arche movement began. *L'Arche* is the French word for "ark" and means the welcoming of all people to live together in community. There are one hundred L'Arche homes throughout the world and the "core members," as the handicapped are called, form the center of each community.

Long Retreat (or Thirty-day Retreat): This is the main experiment of the novitiate. Each Jesuit novice undergoes several experiments during the two-year novitiate to discover whether God is confirming the novice's sense of being called to the Society of Jesus. The Spiritual Exercises take roughly thirty days to complete. Since this is a major time commitment for prayer and solitude, it has come to be known as the "long retreat."

Novice: A novice is a man admitted to the first probation of the Society of Jesus. The Jesuit novice practices living the three vows of chastity, poverty, and obedience in community. He undertakes probationary activities to see if the life suits him and if he suits the life.

Novice director (formerly called novice master): Refers to the mature Jesuit whose role is to work with the novices to discover God's will. The novice director collaborates with a staff to provide spiritual direction, to offer instruction about Jesuit life, and to present the example of a dedicated service to the people of God.

Novitiate: The novitiate is a two-year program of prayer, study, and probations to discover if the candidate for Jesuit life is capable of living in community a vowed life of service for others. Once a man has passed through a stringent screening process, consulted with the Jesuit in charge of recruitment, and interviewed with the novice director, he is admitted into the novitiate. The probations of the novitiate include the Spiritual Exercises, daily prayer and liturgy, discernment in common with the group's apostolic mission, and various other experiences of Jesuit life.

Offertory (or Preparation of Gifts): The transitional phase of the Roman Catholic Mass between the liturgy of the Word and the litury of the Eucharist. Gifts are presented from the people of God, and the priest prepares the bread and wine to be offered on behalf of the people. In Sunday Mass, this is the moment when ushers collect the contributions of those attending Mass.

Omnia Ad Majorem Dei Gloriam (A.M.D.G.): The motto of the Jesuits enunciated by St. Ignatius. It means "Everything for the greater glory of God." The motto indicates the generous desire of the chivalrous heart to strive beyond the requirements of duty in order to achieve the superabundance of love.

Ordination: When a man is chosen by his community for a special service of leadership among the people of God, this designation of service is accomplished in a ceremony that is the culmination of years of prayer, study, and probation. The ceremony is called ordination, because it is an ordering of a man's life to a role within the community. A person may be ordained as a deacon, a priest, or a bishop. Each has a different and specific role of responsibility for the care of the community.

Philosophy: The phase of Jesuit training that formerly followed the humanities study characteristic of the old two-year juniorate and that now follows immediately upon completion of the noviatiate. Jesuits currently begin a three-year program of study after they pronounce their vows. This program entails courses in the history of philosophy and the philosophy of human nature, ethics, knowledge, metaphysics, and God. The theological component encompasses Scripture, doctrine, morality, sacraments, liturgy, and spirituality.

Provincial: The provincial is the Jesuit designated for a period of six years to lead a geographical region of the Society of Jesus. As religious superior, the provincial hears an annual account of conscience from each Jesuit in order to know the man well enough to be able to mission him for the year's service. There are ten provincials in the United States. The provincial of the Oregon province is responsible for Jesuits in Oregon, Washington, Idaho, Montana, and Alaska.

Rector: The Jesuit superior of a local community. Among his responsibilites, he is to pray for his men, to help them accomplish their work, and to direct the spiritual and temporal aspects of his community.

Regency: The phase of Jesuit training that follows philosophical studies but before the theologicial studies that prepare for priesthood. Regency lasts between two to three years. It is a time of active ministry in which the Jesuit student is seen as a public representative of the Church. Regency settings include high school teaching, university instruction, parish service, and Native American ministry.

Isabel Roser: (b: ? d: 1554) A contemporary of St. Ignatius, Isabel Roser provided him with early financial backing. Later, she persuaded Pope Paul III to require Ignatius to allow her to "join" the Jesuits. The experiment proved difficult, and Roser was released from her vows. This experience led Ignatius to refuse to undertake a regular ministry to religious women, and he resolved to admit no other women into the Society of Jesus.

Sheridan: Sheridan is a small farming and logging town in western Oregon and was the site of the Oregon province novitiate from 1932 until the late 1960s, when it relocated to Portland. Sheridan, Oregon, is located fifty-five miles southwest of Portland. The novitiate stood atop a hill on a thousand-acre tract overlooking the Yamhill Valley.

The Spiritual Exercises: When St. Ignatius underwent his own conversion experience during thirteen months of prayer at Manresa in Spain, he discovered a pattern of prayer exercises that aid in freeing a person from disordered attachments and support a person's desire to seek God in all things. This program of prayer, which entails a foundational consideration and four weeks or units of spiritual calisthenics, have come to be known as the Spiritual Exercises of St. Ignatius. The program of prayer is ordinarily conducted under the guidance of a retreat director who is experienced in determining how the Spirit of God is moving in each directee's experience.

Tertianship: From the Latin *tertio*, meaning third, the tertianship is a third year (after the earlier two years of the novitiate) of spiritual formation to elicit great desires for the mission of the

Society. The tertianship refers to the School of the Heart, a year-long program designed to prepare an individual for a life of ministry and the last phase of Jesuit training before the Society invites the Jesuit to pronounce final vows.

Theology: A term that designates the three years of study before ordination to the priesthood. Jesuits from the Oregon province earn the Masters of Divinity degree at one of the Society's North American theological centers: Weston School of Theology in Boston, the Jesuit School of Theology at Berkeley, California, or Regis College in Toronto.

True-friend: This term refers to a relationship of endearment and trust between friends. It is used informally among the Native American tribes of the Northwest.

Two Standards: A standard is a banner carried in battle to designate the location of the commander of the assembled forces. In the *Spiritual Exercises*, one commander reflects on the standard of Christ and the other reflects on the standard of Satan. Ignatius asks us to pay attention to the goals of each, their strategies and allegiances and ways of proceeding. In the thick of battle, Ignatius wants the commander who is praying to choose whether to be placed next to the standard of Christ or to the standard of Satan.

Jean Vanier: (b: 1928) Son of the Governor-General of Canada, Georges Vanier, Jean Vanier was raised in the midst of affluence and privilege. As a layman, and without the benefit of affiliation with any religious group, Vanier founded the L'Arche movement in France in 1964. Now there are one hundred L'Arche homes for emotionally and mentally disabled women and men in twenty-two countries throughout the world. Vanier has written numerous books on community and how a community needs to view the brokenness of each member as the source of healing for the entire group.